AIR CAMPAIGN

# CONTENTS

# INTRODUCTION

A kamikaze crashed on the flight deck of the fleet carrier *Essex* (CV-9) just forward of the Number 2 elevator during attacks on November 25, 1944. (AC)

It had already been one hell of a morning for crews manning the ships of the Seventh Fleet's Task Unit 77.4.1 on October 25, 1944. Best known by its call sign, Taffy 1, it was one of three escort carrier groups providing air cover for US invasion troops on the Leyte beachhead. It consisted of Sangamon-class escort carriers *Sangamon*, *Santee*, and *Suwannee*, Casablanca-class carrier *Petrof Bay*, destroyers *McCord*, *Trathen*, and *Hazelwood*, and destroyer escorts *Edmonds*, *Richard C. Bull*, *Richard M. Rowell*, *Eversole*, and *Coolbaugh*.

A Japanese warship force, including two battleships, had just attempted a failed attack on the Allied invasion fleet off the Leyte Gulf beaches. Most were sunk the previous night in the Surigao Strait by a US battle line guarding the strait, primarily made up of battleships present at Pearl Harbor. As dawn broke, Taffy 1 launched a mixed strike of Hellcat fighters and Avenger torpedo bombers to hunt down the retreating survivors.

One of the first group of kamikaze special attack pilots share a ceremonial cup of sake with Vice Admiral Ōnishi Takijirō, prior to departing on their mission. (USNHHC)

An hour after that strike left, Admiral Thomas Sprague, commanding all three escort carrier groups, present aboard Taffy 1 escort carrier USS *Sangamon*, learned that Taffy 3, 130 miles north, was under attack. Admiral Kurita's Center Force, including *Yamato* and three other battleships, had come through the San Bernardino Strait and were shelling the light-skinned escort carriers, destroyers, and destroyer escorts comprising Taffy 3. Taffy 3's escorts were attacking the Japanese surface ships and its escort carriers were launching aircraft.

They needed help. Thomas Sprague ordered all of Taffy 1 and Taffy 2 to assist Taffy 3. Soon, Taffy 1 was recovering aircraft completing earlier strikes, rearming them, and sending them north to attack the Central Force. At 0729hrs, radar picked up six approaching bogies – unidentified aircraft, potentially hostile. They were identified as bandits – hostile aircraft – six A6M Zeros, known to the Allies as "Zekes."

Tension probably ratcheted down aboard the US carriers. Zekes were fighter aircraft, obsolescent by late 1944, and within the capabilities of Wildcat and Hellcat fighters carried by Taffy 3. Zekes would not be carrying bombs. If they were, they would be small, incapable of doing much damage to an escort carrier with an empty flight deck. Launching the armed and fueled aircraft aboard the carriers became more important, and such operations continued. Two of the six Zeros were subsequently intercepted and destroyed by Taffy 1's combat air patrol.

At 0740hrs, the *Sangamon* was recovering aircraft from the first strike launched to aid Taffy 3. The *Suwannee* and *Petrof Bay* had empty flight decks, while *Santee* had just finished launching five Avengers and eight Wildcats for Taffy 1's second strike against the Central Force. Then four Japanese aircraft were spotted.

A Zero dived out of the clouds at *Santee*. It did not pull out of the dive, smashing into the forward port side of the flight deck, punching through to the hangar deck before the 63kg bomb it was carrying exploded. *Santee* was lucky. The aircraft caused fires near eight 1,000lb bombs, ready munitions for the next airstrike, but they failed to explode. The flames were brought under control within 10 minutes. The attack killed 16 men aboard *Santee* and wounded 27 others.

A Zero dives on USS *Suwannee* to open the kamikaze campaign. This was the first attack in which Allied forces realized the Japanese were conducting intentional suicide attacks. Note the aircraft landing on the carrier. (AC)

Thirty seconds later, two other Zeros dived on the *Suwannee*. Both were shot down; one splashed harmlessly behind the *Suwannee*, while the other closely missed *Petrof Bay*. A fourth Zero was seen, 8,000ft high, circling *Suwannee*. It, too, dived on the carrier. Antiaircraft fire hit that one, too, but it plunged straight into the *Suwannee*, smacking into the flight deck and opening a 10ft hole in the center of the fight deck, 40ft ahead of the aft elevator. The bomb burst between the flight deck and the hangar deck, ripping a 25ft hole in it, exposing the main deck below to daylight. That fire was soon extinguished. By 1009hrs, repairs to the flight deck allowed air operations to resume aboard *Suwannee*.

The attacks had the crews puzzled. Had the four planes intended to crash on the carriers? There was no obvious answer. Pilots of fatally damaged Japanese planes occasionally crashed into their bombing targets. Perhaps the antiaircraft fire had hit the four aircraft, leading the pilots to hit the carriers because they could not get away. A Yokasuka D4Y "Judy" had dropped a bomb on *Petrof Bay* and scooted away immediately after these four planes attacked. Maybe, despite initial appearances, it was not intended as a suicide strike.

Forty minutes later, the US crewmen had their answer. At 1050hrs, Taffy 3, already battered by Kurita's Center Force, reported being under air attack. Five more aircraft deliberately attempted to crash on their targets rather than simply bomb or torpedo them. The escort carrier *St Lo* exploded and sank after being hit by a Zero, while the *White Plains* and *Kalinin Bay* were damaged after other planes crashed on them. Taffy 1 and Taffy 3 had been the first recipients of a new Japanese tactic: the suicide attack.

The aircraft attacking Taffy 1 came from Davao, an airfield on Mindanao in the Philippines. Those attacking Taffy 3 had come from Malabacat Airfield in Luzon. Both belonged to Imperial Japanese Navy (IJN) *tokkotai* units. *Tokko* was an abbreviation of *Tokubetiu Kogeki* – special attack. All units organized to undertake suicide missions, whether by the IJN or Imperial Japanese Army (IJA), were designated *tokkotai*, but *tokkotai* were not limited to aircraft. Land and sea-based *tokkotai* were fielded too.

Aircraft *tokkotai* were the first formally organized *tokkotai*. They were also the most numerous and best known. They were fielded by the IJN under a program it called *kamikaze* (divine wind). The name referred to typhoons which had disrupted two attempted Mongol invasions of Japan in the 13th century. The Navy liked the name, using it for several destroyers.

A Japanese print showing the Mongol fleet being scattered by one of two typhoons in 1274 and 1281. This "Divine Wind" lent the name *kamikaze* to Japanese *tokko* units. (Tokyo National Museum/ Public Domain)

The US capture of the Marianas Islands in summer 1944 had opened the Japanese Home Islands to attack. The military machine forged by the United States and its Pacific allies was grinding relentlessly closer to Japan and invasion. For the Japanese, it appeared 20th-century divine intervention was required to stop this advance. It seemed appropriate for the IJN to invoke the typhoons that scattered the Mongol fleets 700 years earlier with their *tokko* program. The naval air units were called "kamikaze" squadrons.

Although kamikaze was initially only a naval term, the name became associated with all *tokko* efforts, whether Navy or Army. The general public in Japan and the Allied nations called all *tokko* aircraft kamikazes, as did the armed forces of the Allied nations.

*Tokko* seemed an ideal method of countering Allied materiel and personnel superiority. A single aircraft could be exchanged for a major warship or a loaded troop transport. You did not need front-line aircraft – obsolescent ones could be used, since they were not coming back. Even a novice pilot could steer an aircraft into his target. Bombs and torpedoes were unguided after being dropped, and even skilled pilots – which Japan was short of – often missed. The only way to keep a kamikaze aircraft from hitting its target was to shoot it down before it hit, and it seemed impossible for the Allies to shoot down every attacking aircraft.

The effort started as a local initiative in the Philippines, and its initial success in October 1944 led to the program's rapid expansion. The Japanese Navy created a centralized command for its kamikaze units. The Army joined in, creating its own *tokkotai*. Both services instituted kamikaze-training programs and began manufacturing dedicated *tokko* aircraft. The Japanese deployed *tokkotai* in advance of invasions, rapidly transferring additional aircraft after a new Allied incursion; a vast armada of kamikazes was used when the Allies invaded the Home Islands, even to the extent of neglecting the air defense of the Home Islands.

Initially, the Allies had trouble believing the suicide attacks were deliberate. By the end of October 1944, however, they understood the threat posed by kamikazes. Historian Samuel Eliot Morison lived through these attacks during his service in the US Navy. In his history of the United States Navy in World War II, Morison quoted the reaction of a steward's mate a few days after the attacks on Taffy 1 and Taffy 3: "We don't mind them planes which drops things, but we don't like them what *lights* on you."

Once the threat was apparent, the Allies developed countermeasures. The kamikaze threat changed the composition of aircraft carried aboard Allied aircraft carriers during the war's last year. New tactics and strategies were implemented to neutralize them including offensive operations to prevent them from launching missions and a new defensive doctrine.

Over the final 11 months of World War II, both sides were engaged in a struggle with no quarter asked or given. The kamikaze campaign lasted the entire time, dominating both sides' thinking. For Japan, it was literally their last opportunity to avoid unconditional surrender. The extent of Japan's dedication to *tokko* was only apparent after the war's end, when their home defense plans were finally available to the victorious Allies. This book tells that story.

# CHRONOLOGY

## 1944

**September**  Imperial Japanese Navy and Army begin studies to improve aerial effectiveness. Army concludes *tokko* tactics are necessary.

**October**  Admiral Arima Masabumi, commanding First Air Fleet in the Philippines, organizes "Sho" (special attack) units in the Philippines.

**October 15**  Admiral Arima killed attacking US Third Fleet off Formosa.

**October 17**  Admiral Ōnishi Takijirō assumes command of the First Air Fleet.

**October 19**  Admiral Ōnishi organizes first kamikaze unit from 24 volunteers from the 201st Air Group.

**October 25**  First kamikaze attacks are made. Taffy 1 and Taffy 3 attacked by first organized *tokko* units.

**November 11**  IJA begins *tokko* attacks in the Philippines.

**November 30**  Admiral John S. McCain takes command of TF38.

**December 15**  Mindoro in the Philippines invaded by US forces.

## 1945

**January 6**  Lingayan Gulf landings.

**January 22**  Japan withdraws all air forces from the Philippines.

**January 28**  US Third Fleet becomes the Fifth Fleet.

**February 19**  Iwo Jima landings begin.

**February 21–22**  Japanese kamikaze attacks at Iwo Jima.

**February**  Ugaki Matome assigned command of the Fifth Air Fleet in Kyushu and put in charge of all kamikaze attacks against Okinawa.

**March 10**  *Second Tansaku* strike against Ulithi.

**March 18–19**  Fast Carrier Task Force strikes on Japan.

**March 21**  First use of kamikaze Ohkas against Allied carrier forces attacking Okinawa.

**March 26–27**  Kerama Retto occupied.

**April 1**  Main Okinawa invasion begins. Four US infantry divisions land on Hagushi beaches.

**April 6–7**  *Kikusui* 1: 230 IJN and 125 IJA kamikazes participate.

**April 12–13**  *Kikusui* 2: 125 IJN and 60 IJA kamikazes participate.

**April 12**  USS *Mannert L. Abele* becomes first Allied ship sunk by an Ohka bomb.

**April 15–16**  *Kikusui* 3: 120 IJN and 45 IJA kamikazes participate.

**April 16**  Ie Shima invaded and occupied.

**April 27–28**  *Kikusui* 4: 65 IJN and 50 IJA kamikazes participate.

**May 3–4**  *Kikusui* 5: 75 IJN and 50 IJA kamikazes participate.

**May 11–15**  *Kikusui* 6: 70 IJN and 80 IJA kamikazes participate.

**May 23–25**  *Kikusui* 7: 65 IJN and 100 IJA kamikazes participate.

**May 27**  US Fifth Fleet becomes the Third Fleet.

**May 28–29**    *Kikusui* 8: 60 IJN and 50 IJA kamikazes participate.

**June 3–7**    *Kikusui* 9: 20 IJN and 30 IJA kamikazes participate.

**June 21–22**    *Kikusui* 10: 30 IJN and 15 IJA kamikazes participate.

**July 29**    USS *Callahan* becomes the last Allied warship sunk by a kamikaze off Okinawa with a fabric and wood biplane which could not be detected by radar, and including proximity-fuzed shells.

**August 14**    Japan surrenders.

**August 15**    Ugaki Matome dies in a kamikaze mission flown to preclude surrender.

**August 15**    Ōnishi Takijirō commits *seppuku*.

**November 1**    Planned Operation *Olympic* landing date.

**1946**
**March 1**    Planned Operation *Coronet* landing date.

Antiaircraft fire was the final line of defense against kamikazes. This shows the pattern of antiaircraft fire during kamikaze attacks off the Hagushi beaches shortly after sunset on April 27, 1945. (AC)

# ATTACKER'S CAPABILITIES
## The last of Japanese airpower

The kamikaze campaign was an example of an offensive shaped by the resources and capabilities of the Japanese attackers, who were limited by available aircraft, airfields, and weapons. It was also an expensive campaign in terms of resources consumed. There was a tacit acceptance that pilots and aircraft had become consumable goods, along with more traditional materiel such as munitions and fuel. Logistics and reserves played an important role in replacing expended resources. Once reserves were used, replacements had to be found. This included manufacturing aircraft and training pilots for exclusive kamikaze duty.

The capabilities of the aircraft used, the aircrew supporting the kamikaze campaign, and the effectiveness of the weapons deployed all affected the chances of success, but so too did the infrastructure available to the Japanese. This included the airfields from which aircraft flew and the support system maintaining, fueling, and arming the aircraft used.

Additionally, Japan developed dedicated weapons for kamikaze use, both in the form of aircraft and warheads. Kamikaze attacks required the development of dedicated tactics, to maximize the chance of a hit and the damage inflicted.

However, Japan's success or failure during the kamikaze campaign would be due to more than the capabilities of its aircraft, facilities and infrastructure, and weapons and tactics individually. It would also depend upon the capability Japan had to integrate these elements to work together so that individual weaknesses were compensated by strengths elsewhere. Japan needed to operate the kamikazes as part of a system, a capability where it was weak.

## Aircraft

Any aircraft capable of carrying explosives could be used as a kamikaze, and almost every type of aircraft was during this campaign. High-performance fighters, single- and twin-engine bombers, transports, and trainers all saw use as kamikazes. Cloth-and-wood biplanes were pressed into kamikaze service. Japan even manufactured aircraft as dedicated suicide aircraft,

The Mitsubishi A6M Zero started out the Pacific War as the conflict's most effective fighter. By 1944 it was obsolescent, outclassed by newer Allied fighters. Its speed and maneuverability made it an outstanding kamikaze aircraft. (AC)

such as the Ohka suicide rocket. Kamikaze aircraft were defined by their guidance system: a pilot intent on crashing a bomb-laden aircraft into a target. Only four-engine flying boats and some twin-engine Mitsubishi G4Ms were spared kamikaze duty.

The former were bypassed because they were so large and slow that there was no chance they would score a hit. The latter were spared largely so they could launch Ohkas, but Japan even had plans to use those when the Allies invaded the Home Islands. War plans intended to use every flyable aircraft as a kamikaze: a minimum of three-quarters of available aircraft were to repel the invasion of Kyushu, with any survivors to defend Honshu. Yet certain aircraft were commonly used as kamikazes, others rarely, and a few were manufactured as kamikazes.

The Mitsubishi A6M was the most commonly used kamikaze aircraft. Nearly 650 were sent, a number greater than the three next most-used aircraft: the Nakajima Ki-43, Yokosuka D4Y1, and Kawasaki Ki-61 combined. At least 200 of each of these were expended as kamikazes. All were single-engine fighters and bombers.

The Yokosuka P1Y1, Nakajima Ki-27, Nakajima Ki-84, and Aichi D3A formed a third cohort. Between 125 and 175 of each aircraft were used. Nearly 100 Kawasaki Ki-61s were used, as were around 80 Nakajima B5Ns torpedo bombers and 65 Kawasaki Ki-45 fighters. The P1Y1 and Ki-45 were twin-engine aircraft, whereas the others were single-engine models.

Twenty-one other types of Japanese aircraft were expended on kamikaze missions in numbers ranging from just one to 50. In all, over 2,500 aircraft and their crews were sacrificed to the Thunder Gods.

**Mitsubishi A6M (Zero, or Allied code name Zeke, Hamp):** This was the infamous Mitsubishi *Reisen* (Zero) that dominated the Pacific in 1941 and 1942. By late 1944, however, it was hopelessly outclassed by new Allied fighters, especially the F6F Hellcat and F4U Corsair. Zeros were armed with two 7.7mm machine guns and two 20mm cannon, had a 32,000ft service ceiling, a 1,600nmi range, and a 332mph top speed. Zeros used as kamikazes were fitted with a 250kg (550lb) bomb. Zeros also provided kamikazes with fighter escort.

**Aichi D3A (Val):** This fixed-gear monoplane was Japan's standard dive bomber through most of the war. Obsolescent, it was to have been replaced by 1943, but problems with its replacement kept the D3A in service. It had a top speed of 267mph, cruised at 184mph, had a 34,500ft ceiling, and an 840nmi range. It carried one 250kg (551lb) bomb.

**Nakajima B5N (Kate):** This was the Imperial Japanese Navy's standard carrier-based torpedo bomber at the start of World War II. The **Nakajima B6N Tenzan (Heavenly Mountain,** or **Jill)** was its replacement. As kamikazes, both carried up to 800kg (1,760lb) in bombs. The B5N had a top speed of 235mph, a cruising speed of 161mph, a ceiling of 27,000ft, and a 1,200nmi range. The B6N had a top speed of 300mph, a ceiling of 29,660ft, and 934nmi combat range.

**Nakajima Ki-43 Hayabusa (Peregrine Falcon,** or **Oscar):** The Japanese Army's standard fighter when the war began. A single-engine, low-wing monoplane, it carried either two 7.7mm machine guns, two 12.7mm machine guns, or two 20mm cannon, depending

While other twin-engine bombers were used for kamikaze duties, almost no Mitsubishi G4Ms were, largely due to their usefulness in carrying the Yokosuka MXY-7 Ohka bomb. This G4M is preparing for a mission carrying an Ohka. (USNHHC)

on the version. As a kamikaze, it carried two 250kg underwing bombs. It had a 330mph top speed, a 26,700ft ceiling, and 950nmi combat range.

**Mitsubishi G4M (Betty):** This played a prominent role in the kamikaze campaign as a carrier for the Ohka flying bomb. A twin-engine aircraft, it had a top speed of 365mph, a cruising speed of 196mph, and a 1,770nmi range. However, it was so notorious for catching fire after being hit that its crews called it the "Type 1 cigarette lighter."

As the campaign continued, aircraft types were committed as kamikazes expanded. The Japanese Navy occasionally employed the **Yokosuka P1Y Ginga (Galaxy, or Francis)**, a twin-engine, land-based bomber, as a kamikaze. With its top speed of 340mph, a range of 2,900nmi, and a ceiling of 30,000ft, it was fast enough to evade fighters and could strike across unexpectedly long distances, carrying up to 1,000kg (2,200lb). So was

the **Yokosuka D4Y1 (Judy)** dive, reconnaissance, and level bomber. Fast (a 342mph maximum speed), with a range of 910 miles and a 35,000ft service ceiling, it could carry 1,000lb of bombs.

By the middle of the Okinawa phase of the kamikaze campaign, many of the aircraft used on *tokko* missions were obsolescent types, such as this Kawasaki Ki-32 Type 98 light bomber. Since they were not expected to survive a mission, they were sent on one-way trips to attack the enemy. (AC)

The Japanese Army also used a wide variety of aircraft as kamikazes. While the Hayabusa was used, so were virtually any fast nimble aircraft capable of carrying a bomb. Probably the next most commonly used Army suicide aircraft was the **Mitsubishi Ki-51 (Sonya).** A two-seat, low-winged, single-engine monoplane with fixed landing gear, it had been the Army's primary prewar light bomber. Retired to training duties, it was brought back to combat status for suicide missions. It had a 263mph top speed, 27,130ft ceiling, and 570nmi range. It carried two forward-firing and one flexible rear-firing 7.7mm machine guns. It carried one 550kg bomb on suicide duty.

The Army also used the **Nakajima Ki-27 (Nate), Kawasaki Ki-61 Hien (Flying Swallow, or Tony)**, and **Nakajima Ki-84 Hayate (Gale, or Frank)** as suicide airplanes. All were low-wing single-engine fighters. The Ki-27, a prewar design with fixed landing gear, was a trainer during the Pacific War. As with the Ki-51, its combat career resumed as a kamikaze. The Hien and Hayate were both first-line fighters usually used to escort kamikazes. As the campaign progressed, they too were used for kamikaze missions. When used as kamikazes, they would carry one bomb, weighing 200kg and 500kg respectively.

The Army used biplane trainers such as the Tachikawa Ki-9 and Kokusai Ki-105 as kamikazes. Although unarmed, these could carry a 100–200kg bomb in the second seat. Due to their wood-and-fabric construction, they were hard to spot on radar. They proved surprisingly effective, despite their slow speed.

The most extensive Army *tokko* conversions involved the twin-engine **Kawasaki Ki-48 Type 99 twin-engined light bomber (Lily)** and **Mitsubishi Ki-67 *Hiryu* Type IV heavy bomber (Flying Dragon, or Peggy)**. In August 1944, the Imperial Japanese Army armed 12 of each with a contact fuze and massive bomb load. The Ki-48s carried one 800kg demolition bomb, while the Ki-67 held two. Both were fast, capable machines: the Ki-48 had a top speed of 314mph and a range of 1,300nmi, while the Ki-67 could reach 334mph, cruise at 250mph, and had a combat range of 1,500nmi.

**OPPOSITE** STRATEGIC OVERVIEW

The Japanese also developed dedicated suicide attack aircraft. The best known was the infamous **Yokosuka MXY-7 Ohka** (**Cherry blossom**, or "Baka" or "fool" to the Allies). Rocket-powered, Ohkas could reach 400mph in level flight or 580mph in a dive, making them virtually immune to fighter interception. The nose was filled with a 1,200kg (2,600lb) Ammonal warhead. With only a 20nmi range, it had to be carried to the battlefield under a bomber and dropped near its target.

First flown in October 1944, the Ohka became operational in 1945. Over 750 were built before the war ended. Relatively few were used operationally during World War II, all during the battle for Okinawa. Ohkas sank only one ship and damaged four others, but captured the imagination of their foes. Ground-launched versions were developed for defense in the event of an invasion of Japan, but never used operationally.

The **Nakajima Ki-115 Tsurugi** (or **Sabre**), or **Tōka (Wisteria Blossom)** was another purpose-built kamikaze aircraft. A low-wing, single-engine monoplane with fixed landing gear jettisoned after takeoff, it had a simple and cheap design, intended to supplement the obsolete aircraft available for the defense of Japan. It had a 340mph top speed, a 650nmi range, and no armament except a single 250kg, 500kg, or 800kg bomb. Tsurugi was the Army's name for the Ki-115; Tōka the Navy's. Before Japan's surrender ended construction, 105 were built. None were used operationally, but would have been if the war had continued.

## Facilities and infrastructure

Supporting the kamikaze campaign was a network of airfields Japan owned or had conquered or built since the start of the Pacific War. Both the Japanese Army and Navy had numerous airfields in conquered territories such as the Philippines, and pre-war Japanese holdings like Formosa, from which kamikazes could operate. Among these were highly developed airfields with paved runways, including the captured Clark Field in the Philippines and Tainan Airfield in Formosa. There were also many unimproved fields with grass airstrips and rudimentary fueling facilities, such as Mabalacat East and West Airfields in the Philippines, from where the first kamikaze missions originated.

The needs of most kamikaze aircraft were simple. Clearly, long-term maintenance was unimportant, so long as an aircraft was mechanically fit enough to take off and reach its target. Fuel, lubricants, and bombs were their only logistical needs. Most kamikaze

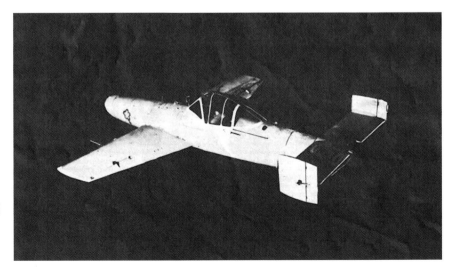

The kamikaze weapon probably most feared by the Allies was the rocket-powered Ohka flying bomb. A manned missile, it was virtually unstoppable once launched, as it outran Allied fighters and provided only a small target for antiaircraft artillery, even when firing proximity fuze munitions. (AC)

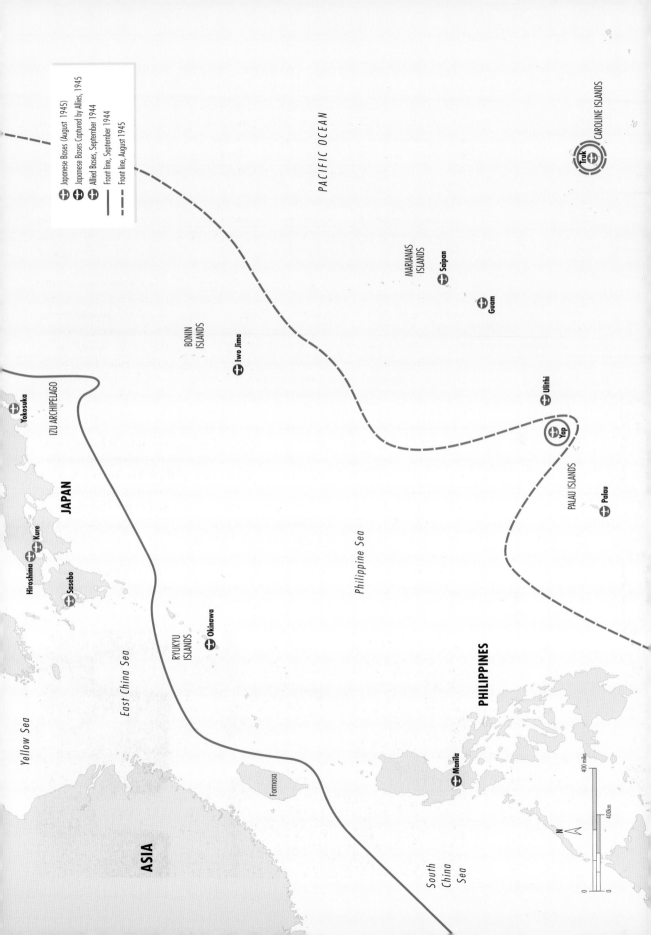

**Japanese Bases (August 1945)**
**Japanese Bases Captured by Allies, 1945**
**Allied Bases, September 1944**
Front line, September 1944
Front line, August 1945

PACIFIC OCEAN

CAROLINE ISLANDS

Truk

MARIANAS
ISLANDS
Saipan

Guam

BONIN
ISLANDS
Iwo Jima

Ulithi

Yap

PALAU ISLANDS

Palau

Yokosuka

IZU ARCHIPELAGO

JAPAN

Kure

Hiroshima

Sasebo

RYUKYU
ISLANDS
Okinawa

Philippine Sea

East China Sea

Yellow Sea

ASIA

Formosa

PHILIPPINES

Manila

South
China
Sea

N

400 miles

400km

aircraft were single-engine aircraft. They could use widely dispersed grass fields, striking when needed.

This worked initially in the Philippines, with numerous available fields. However, once the Allies were familiar with kamikazes, they developed an effective strategy to counter them – they shut down every enemy airfield within range of Allied tactical aircraft. When Luzon was invaded, none of the Philippine airfields could effectively stage kamikaze strikes. The only kamikaze attacks on the Allied invasion fleet at Lingayen originated from Formosa, across the Luzon Strait, out of range of Allied tactical aircraft.

Using dispersed bases for kamikaze attacks was less useful in the Iwo Jima and Okinawa phases of the kamikaze campaign due to the smaller geographical size of those areas. Allied fast carriers had enough aircraft to use smothering tactics on all of the airfields on those islands prior to invasion. Most of the kamikazes deployed in those phases came from remote bases, generally originating in the Home Islands.

In the final defense of Japan, dispersed airfields would have regained utility. The size of Kyushu and Honshu precluded Allied forces smothering all possible airfields, much less pre-positioned kamikazes concealed at unimproved launch sites for a one-time strike.

More successful was the use of remote airfields as kamikaze bases. Long-range bombers, attacking from remote distances, found it difficult to shut down kamikaze airfields. B-29s used for this found empty airfields when they arrived. Flying from the Marianas to hit Japanese airfields in Kyushu gave Japanese radio intelligence and radar several hours of warning, allowing aircraft to be evacuated. After the raids, damaged runways were quickly patched and the airfields were often operating again before the B-29s returned home.

Japan at this stage lacked sufficient pilots capable of carrier operations, so no kamikaze flight originated from aircraft carriers. The only role Japanese carriers played during the kamikaze campaign was as aircraft ferries, transporting kamikaze aircraft to forward bases. Several, including the *Shinano* and *Unryu*, were lost on these missions.

The limiting factor on kamikaze missions through August 1945 was the availability of pilots. Aviation gasoline shortages, which got worse as the campaign continued, limited pilot training prior to October 1944, creating increasing restrictions as the campaign continued. Both Japanese Army and Navy flight training was also constricted by the small number of

Kamikaze aircraft take off from a grass-runway auxiliary airfield near Manila in the Philippines. The kamikazes' ability to operate from any airfield, including unimproved facilities, magnified the threat they posed. (USNHHC)

flight schools. At the start of the Pacific War, the Navy was producing only 2,000 pilots a year, while the Army added just 750. Both expanded training enormously during World War II, the Army increasing its flight schools from 18 to 48. By 1944, each service was turning out 2,700 pilots annually, a total of 5,400.

Training time fell precipitously, however. In 1941, Japanese Navy pilots received 700 hours of flight training; Army pilots 500. By late 1944, this had shrunk to about 300 and 150, respectively. Three hundred hours was adequate – even US Navy aviators only received 300 hours of flying time prior to seeing combat. But 150 hours did not provide enough time to create an effective combat pilot.

Training time plunged after October 1944. By August 1945, Japanese Navy and Army pilots were receiving only 100 hours of flight time before being committed to combat. There was insufficient available gasoline for more. The Army's training problem was magnified because many of the expansion flight schools were in the Philippines. Established there to shorten the distance from Indonesian fuel sources, these bases were lost following Allied landings on Leyte.

Pilots trained exclusively as kamikazes received even less training, often only 30–50 flight hours. Their training was abbreviated, focusing on takeoff and flight; gunnery, navigation, and instrument-flying training were minimized. As spring 1945 opened, all conventional flight training ended. Flight schools then concentrated exclusively on training kamikazes.

Another issue was an adequate supply of men willing to serve as *tokko* pilots. Initially this was not a problem as the opening of the kamikaze campaign used limited numbers to test the concept. There was, at this stage, a surplus of volunteers, to the point where commanders had to stop "ride-alongs" on missions in which more than one qualified pilot rode aboard a kamikaze. Nevertheless, the campaign's continuation and expansion soon exhausted the pool of willing, well-trained volunteers. Competent veteran pilots had to be reserved for supporting flights, both to fly fighter escort and man bombers carrying Ohkas. Although those intent on kamikaze service generally found a way to serve, soon badly trained and ultimately untrained volunteers were accepted for kamikaze duty. "Volunteers" were often coerced; shamed into volunteering or simply ordered to volunteer. Officially, this did not happen; in practice, it did.

One of the paradoxes of the kamikaze campaign was that, as the campaign progressed, the attackers were constantly retreating as their supply lines shrank. This simplified logistics but resources were limited. At the start of the kamikaze campaign, Japan's industrial infrastructure was intact, working at its greatest capacity of the war, but by the end, it

The *Shinano*, Japan's largest aircraft carrier, was sunk on its maiden voyage from Yokosuka Naval Arsenal to Kure Naval Base in November 1944. It was ferrying 50 Yokosuka MXY7 Ohkas when sunk. The loss delayed the operational introduction of the Ohka until 1945. (USNHHC)

was in collapse. The B-29 campaign against the Japanese homeland began in November 1944 and, although largely ineffective before March 1945, it found its measure and rapidly destroyed Japan's industrial base. Japan also relied on an intricate network of imports from throughout its empire and lost most of its strategic imports of rubber, petroleum, and non-ferrous metals in January 1945, when its supply lines to the East Indies and Southeast Asia were severed. Imports from Formosa, including alcohol used in high-octane fuels, ceased shortly afterwards. Thereafter, Japan depended upon stockpiles – until these stockpiles were destroyed by bombing. Sea mines cut off supplies from Manchukuo soon after that, starving Japanese industry still further.

Supplies and materiel to support the campaign grew increasingly tight as it continued, but there always remained enough aircraft, bombs, and fuel to conduct all the kamikaze flights desired, and enough obsolescent and operational aircraft existed for use in kamikaze service through November 1945. Because Japan prioritized kamikazes ahead of all other defense measures, increasing its priority as the war continued, the campaign was never short of resources. Indeed, Japan's conventional forces were cannibalized to feed the kamikazes. Shortages of aircraft and fuel may have arisen had the war continued until March 1946. The plan, had the war carried on, was to use half of the surviving air resources for kamikazes. Everything flyable – and much that was not – was to be thrown against the enemy, half of them in suicide attacks. A postwar review of Japanese plans revealed the government expected to use 5,250 aircraft, three-quarters of which were trainers, as kamikazes.

## Weapons and tactics

The nature of a kamikaze dictated that the primary weapon system of the kamikaze campaign was the aircraft itself. Two components of this weapon merit further examination: the guidance system and the warhead.

The best way to consider a kamikaze is as a cruise missile or precision-guided munition with a human being substituting for a digital computer as the guidance system. This overcame one of the biggest weaknesses of World War II-era bombs and torpedoes, which were uncontrolled after separation from the aircraft carrying them. Ballistics and waves determined their trajectories, allowing targets to evade them; a guided warhead followed the target, nullifying evasion.

During World War II, Nazi Germany and the US introduced a man into the guidance loop using a camera on the guided warhead, with radio communication allowing a pilot to fly the vehicle remotely. These weapons had some success, most notably the September 1943 sinking of the Italian battleship *Roma* by a German Fritz-X radio-guided bomb. However, their effectiveness was limited by radio jamming and vacuum tube electronics. (Note: frequency-hopping and solid-state electronics turned precision-guided munitions into deadly weapons by the 1990–91 Gulf War.) Japan, seeking a cheaper, simpler, and more reliable solution, substituted a human pilot for electronics and radios. For troops to commit suicide in such a systematic and certain fashion would have been unthinkable in a Western society (although the Nazis and Soviets flirted with suicide tactics, and even in the West volunteers on many high-risk missions *expected* to die). But it fitted within the ethos of Imperial Japan's Bushido culture. The Imperial Rescript to Soldiers and Sailors, memorized by all Imperial Japanese military personnel, stated: "Duty is heavier than a mountain; death is lighter than a feather." Yet even they found limits on the numbers willing to serve in such a manner.

Even the most willing human guidance system had limitations, especially as the campaign progressed. The lack of training limited the skill of the later pilots. Lack of instrument-flying training reduced night attacks or attacks in poor visibility, which would have made kamikazes more difficult to intercept. Possessing only rudimentary flying skills, they were easier for the experienced Allied pilots to shoot down. Moreover, the kamikaze pilots lacked ship-recognition skills, being unable to distinguish between an escort or a fleet carrier. Often they struck the first ship spotted, frequently an easily replaced radar picket destroyer or destroyer escort, instead of pressing on to the main body.

Most kamikazes carried a 250kg (551lb) bomb as a warhead. This was on the light side for sinking a ship with a single hit; Allied dive bombers routinely carried 1,000lb or 2,000lb bombs when attacking major warships. Allied aircraft used 500lb bombs when skip bombing (bombs skimming across the top of the water) or mast-top bombing, but depended on multiple hits in such attacks to sink a vessel.

The aircraft and its fuel contributed to the damage caused by a kamikaze. Aircraft construction, which minimized structural weight, gave them little penetrating power. An aircraft could rip through a wooden carrier, but generally failed to penetrate a metal deck. The crush space in the aircraft decelerated the bomb attached,

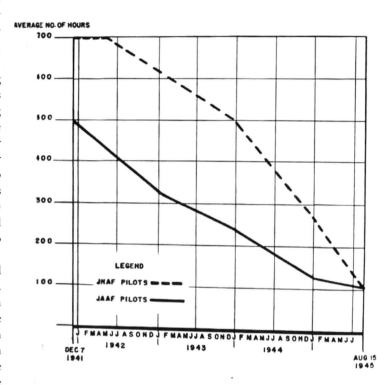

### DECREASE IN PILOT FLYING EXPERIENCE IN JNAF AND JAAF

1941————1945

reducing its penetration to that of the aircraft. Indeed, fire from burning fuel often did more damage than the airplane or bomb carried.

The resulting damage from a kamikaze hit was confined to a ship's upper decks: the flight deck or hangar deck of a carrier, or the weather decks of a surface warship. The result was spectacular but survivable damage to a ship's upper levels, with fire as the greatest danger. Only Ohkas which hit at a high speed, with the warhead in the nose, were likely to penetrate into a ship's bowels and damage watertight integrity.

Ironically, the only fast carrier sunk during the kamikaze campaign was USS *Princeton*, hit by a conventional bomb dropped by a dive bomber. It penetrated the hangar deck, exploding deep in the ship, where burning gasoline complicated firefighting and cooked-off ammunition in the ship's magazine. The same bomb, carried by a kamikaze, would have exploded on the hangar deck, creating less opportunity for gasoline to leak deep into the ship.

Japanese planners, realizing this limitation, were trying to eliminate it. Trainers being prepared for kamikaze duties during the defense of Japan had a bomb rack installed beneath the fuselage so that pilots could, in theory, release a bomb just before hitting their target. Without the plane to retard its speed, the bomb would have greater penetrating power.

Japan developed tactics specifically for kamikaze use, tactics which evolved over the course of the campaign. Initial sorties involved only five or six aircraft; three were kamikazes, while the remaining were escorting fighters to protect the kamikazes from enemy aircraft. The approach exploited known weaknesses in Allied radar coverage. SK air search radar was prone to self-interference from reflection off land or sea surfaces, and also had gaps directly

One reason Japan felt compelled to resort to *tokko* tactics was the lack of pilots skilled enough to complete conventional missions. Japan could not replace combat losses with trained replacements, and training time fell precipitously in late 1944 and into 1945. (AC)

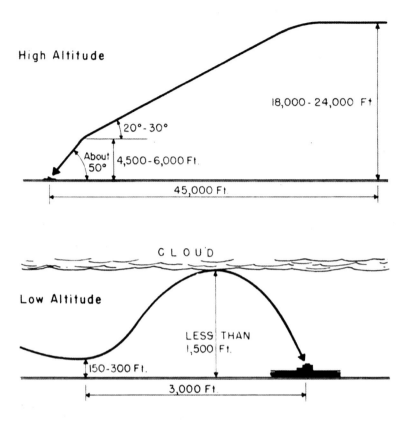

**High Altitude**

18,000 - 24,000 Ft

20° - 30°

About 50°   4,500 - 6,000 Ft.

45,000 Ft.

C L O U D

**Low Altitude**

LESS THAN 1,500 Ft.

150 - 300 Ft.

3,000 Ft.

Japan developed specific tactics to conduct kamikaze attacks, including means of attacking ships from either high or low altitudes. Both were designed to minimize the effectiveness of Allied antiaircraft fire. (AC)

overhead. Centimeter SM and SP radars, meanwhile, used for fighter direction, lacked range for air search. Consequently, kamikazes approached at extremely low or high altitudes to evade detection, and would also trail returning Allied airstrikes to try to sneak in undetected.

Upon sighting carriers, the kamikazes split up, attacking from different directions and choosing varying targets. High-altitude kamikazes would dive at an initial 20–30 degree angle, increasing to a 50 degree dive during terminal approach. Low-altitude aircraft would climb to 1,500ft or so when within 1,000 yards of a target, and then dive into the ship.

Initially, especially among IJN kamikazes, highest target priority was given to aircraft carriers, followed by battleships and cruisers. Army pilots were directed to aim for large transports, reflecting the Army's desire to reduce enemy troops prior to landing. When attacking carriers, pilots were directed to aim for the elevators. These were highly visible, and hard to repair if damaged. The forward elevator was preferred.

Pilots were directed to avoid the island, as hitting that only created superficial damage. In all cases, pilots were told to aim at the center of the ship and attack from abeam to maximize the chance of a hit. They were also directed to keep their eyes open lest they miss the target and to shout just before hitting the ship.

The initial round of kamikaze sorties depended on stealth and surprise to evade Allied air cover. Small numbers were used in the hope of slipping through undetected. As the Allies developed countermeasures, this proved less successful. Another problem was the loss of trained pilots and their replacement by half-trained novices. To compensate, larger strikes were dispatched. However, mass attacks involving hundreds of aircraft were never attempted; there were too few skilled pilots available to attempt to saturate Allied air defenses in this manner. Assembling a mass formation required formation flying skills lacked by the novice pilots available, and they were likewise unable to conduct close-interval takeoffs. Instead, formations of between 12 and 22 aircraft would be dispatched over the course of a day. This resulted in mass attacks taking place during the entire day – or several days during the Okinawa phase. Since these pilots lacked navigation skills, flying from Kyushu they found the US Third Fleet by following the Ryukyu chain from one island to the next.

Saturation kamikaze tactics might have been employed to repel a US invasion of Japan, however. There were many more runways available (including improvised ones to improve dispersal) and the enemy forces would have been close offshore, simplifying the task of finding them. It would have been straightforward to launch multiple if uncoordinated strikes in the hope of overwhelming Allied combat air patrols.

# DEFENDER'S CAPABILITIES
## The encroaching fleet

The Allies' response to the threat posed by the kamikaze campaign was defined by the capabilities of their aircraft, the support infrastructure they possessed, and the weapons they had plus the tactics they developed to counter the kamikaze threat.

The United States and its allies fought the campaign with the resources that had been developed to allow Allied ground forces to invade and hold Japanese-held territory, and eventually the Japanese Home Islands. They had to marshal these existing resources and capabilities to stop the kamikazes, while simultaneously supporting their original objectives. Individual capabilities meant little, used in isolation; they had to be forged into an integrated system. This was done over the course of the kamikaze campaign, quickly and spontaneously, to meet this new threat. In a sense, the ability to meld the capabilities of individual parts of the Allies' operational system – aircraft, antiaircraft, radar, and logistics – to defeating the kamikazes proved to be the Allies' most important skill. It was also one of the hardest to capture and define.

The Grumman F6F Hellcat was the US Navy's primary carrier fighter from 1943 through to the end of the war. Designed to best the Zero, it served admirably as an air superiority fighter and was the kamikazes' primary opponent. (AC)

### Aircraft

A wide variety of aircraft were used by the United States and its allies during the kamikaze campaign. Bombers, including the B-29, were used to attempt to close airfields from which kamikazes flew. However, except when used in conjunction with "Big Blue Blanket" tactics, which involved fighters providing continuous air cover over Japanese airfields while bombers dropped parachute-retarded fragmentation ("parafrag") bombs during intervals when the fighters were changing shifts, bombing airfields proved largely ineffective. The Allied side of the kamikaze campaign was primarily a fighter show.

Virtually all aerial kamikaze attacks were conducted against ships, usually in the aftermath of an invasion landing. USAAF fighters could not participate until land-based airfields were then opened, and these were generally unavailable when kamikaze activity was greatest. Even then, the USAAF was ill-equipped to provide combat air patrol over ships at sea.

The Vought F4U Corsair was superior to the Hellcat as both a fighter and fighter-bomber. It was also significantly more difficult to operate off aircraft carriers. Prior to 1945, it was largely used with squadrons operating from land bases, but thereafter more were being assigned to carriers. (AC)

That required specialized skills that USAAF pilots rarely developed. Consequently, most of the fighters combating the kamikaze threat were from the US Navy and Fleet Air Arm.

Three naval fighter aircraft carried the primary burden against the kamikazes: the Grumman F6F, the Vought F4U, and the Supermarine Seafire. Three other Grumman fighters – the F4F, F7F, and F8F – played subsidiary roles. Additionally, the Grumman Avenger and Curtiss Helldiver had supporting roles in keeping Japanese airfields closed when the Fast Carrier Task Force smothered them with the Big Blue Blanket.

**Grumman F6F Hellcat:** Appearing in late 1943, the Hellcat was designed to provide superiority over the Zero, and proved highly effective against successor Japanese fighters. It ended the war as the Allies' most cost-effective fighter, as measured by the cost of the aircraft compared to the number of enemy aircraft downed. By 1944, it was the US Navy's primary carrier-based fighter, and remained so through 1945. By 1945, it was also being used as a fighter-bomber, carrying up to 4,000lb of bombs (although 1,000–2,000lb was more typical). It could carry up to six 5in. rockets and had six .50cal machine guns. It had a top speed of 391mph, cruising speed of 200mph, service ceiling of 37,300ft, and a range of 1,300 nautical miles. There were also radar-equipped night fighter versions available by 1944, which were used extensively.

Hellcats involved in the kamikaze campaign operated exclusively off aircraft carriers, both US and British. When the campaign started, fleet carriers fielded one Hellcat squadron of between 32 and 38 fighters, a light carrier held one squadron of 22–24 Hellcats, while escort carriers with Hellcats carried between 18 and 22. Due to kamikaze attacks, the US Navy increased the number of fighters carried to a minimum of 52 and a maximum of 75. The Royal Navy also used Hellcats with the British Pacific Fleet aircraft carriers present during the kamikaze campaign, most notably aboard HMS *Indomitable*.

**Vought F4U Corsair:** Bigger and more powerful than the Hellcat, the Corsair had a longer gestation period. It first flew in 1940, but was not fielded on US carriers until after the Hellcat. The Corsair was a single-engine fighter, armed with six .50cal machine guns. It had a top speed of 417mph, cruise speed of 220mph, service ceiling of 36,000ft, and a 1,000nmi range. It was the first US fighter aircraft to exceed 400mph. It, too, was used as a fighter-bomber, often carrying 4,000lb of bombs. It could also carry eight 5in. rockets. The Corsair was initially manufactured by Vought, but was later produced by Goodyear and Brewster. Although identical to the Vought aircraft, Goodyear Corsairs were FGs under the US Navy's aircraft designation system, while Brewster models were F3As.

As Corsairs proved difficult to land on aircraft carriers, they were temporarily withdrawn from carrier service, instead being used by land-based US Navy and Marine Corps squadrons. However, as the Corsair was faster and more powerful than the Hellcat, it was soon reintroduced to carrier service. In early 1944, radar-equipped night fighter Corsairs were assigned to carriers in limited numbers, typically with four per fleet carrier. By February 1945, Corsair day fighter squadrons began operating off US fleet carriers. Two carriers had 36-aircraft Corsair squadrons at Iwo Jima, and the numbers increased thereafter. The British Pacific Fleet also fielded Corsairs aboard HMS *Victorious* and HMS *Illustrious* during the kamikaze campaign, carrying 36 on each carrier.

**Supermarine Seafire:** The Seafire was a single-seat, single-engine fighter used by the Royal Navy, a navalized version of the Spitfire with folding wings. It had a top speed of 359mph, cruising speed of 272mph, service ceiling of 36,000ft, and a 400nmi range. Armed with two 20mm cannon and four .303 Browning machine guns, it could also carry eight 60lb rockets or 500lb of bombs. An outstanding air-superiority fighter, it had excellent performance at high altitude, but only a short range.

Forty Seafires were carried by HMS *Indomitable* and 48 on HMS *Implacable* during the kamikaze campaign. Their high rate of climb and excellent high-altitude performance made Seafires valuable in close-in fleet air defense, despite the limited numbers in which they were fielded.

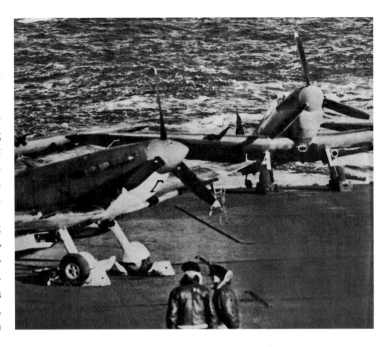

The Seafire's excellent climb rate and high-altitude performance, combined with its short range, led to its use protecting fleet carrier groups. The Seafire provided a valuable counter to the kamikaze threat. (AC)

**Grumman F4F and FM Wildcat:** This was the US Navy's primary fleet fighter when World War II began. It held its own against the superior Japanese Zero, but was superseded by the F6F in 1943. The Wildcat was rugged and reliable, with more forgiving takeoff and landing characteristics than the Hellcat. It was used by most escort carriers, typically with 14–16 carried. Intended for antisubmarine or ground support duties, it frequently defended escort carrier units against kamikaze attacks. Armed with four .50cal machine guns, it had a top speed of 331mph, cruised at 155mph, had a service ceiling of 39,500ft, and a 700nmi range. Wildcats manufactured by General Motors were designated FMs.

**Grumman F7F Tigercat and F8F Bearcat:** The Tigercat and Bearcat arrived in the summer of 1945, both playing minimal roles in the kamikaze campaign after June 1945. They saw limited use in the final two months of the war during a lull in kamikaze activities. They would have played an important role countering kamikazes during Operation *Downfall*, the proposed invasion of Japan, had it occurred.

The Tigercat was a two-seat, twin-engine heavy fighter intended to operate off the large Midway-class carriers, two of which were commissioned in fall 1945. The Tigercat was armed with four 20mm cannon and four .50cal machine guns, with a top speed of 460mph, service ceiling of 40,400ft, and range of 1,000nmi. It was flown largely by the Marine Corps, from land bases. A radar-equipped version, used as a night fighter, replaced the .50cal machine guns with a radar set.

The Bearcat, a single engine, single seat fighter, was smaller than the Hellcat, but faster than any other Navy fighter except the Tigercat. Armed with either four .50cal machine guns (F8F-1) or four 20mm cannon (F8F-1B and later), it had a top speed of 455mph, ceiling of 40,800ft, and range of 920nmi. It was the final single piston-engine aircraft of World War II. The first Bearcat squadron became operational in May 1945, but did not see combat before the war ended.

## Facilities and infrastructure

The Allies' Pacific War strategic goal was to invade and occupy Japan, which required projecting power across the Pacific Ocean. Tokyo was nearly 4,500nmi from San Francisco,

The fleet aircraft carrier – especially the 14 Essex-class carriers available during the kamikaze campaign, such as the one shown here – allowed the Allies to project air power throughout the Pacific. By 1945, Allied fast-carrier task groups routinely operated nearly 1,000 aircraft during operations. (AC)

over 4,200nmi from Sydney, Australia, and 5,700nmi from India's east coast. The United States alone had 30-plus US Army divisions and six US Marine divisions in the Pacific Theater, each infantry division consuming 1,600 tons of supplies a day. British and Commonwealth land forces magnified the burden still more.

By summer 1944, the Allies had mastered moving supplies for these ground troops and to the supply ships, warships, warplanes, and bases required to support them. A large, coordinated logistic system supported a massive military machine across the breadth of the Pacific. Supplies moved to advance bases in the Marianas and Caroline Islands. Thereafter, logistics went seaborne. An armada of transports and cargo ships accompanied troops invading Japanese-held territory, and could supply landed troops for weeks – by the time of the Okinawa landings for months – from floating bases. This placed a large, static, and vulnerable floating infrastructure within reach of enemy attack.

Many invasion beaches were too far from Allied bases for land-based aircraft to provide tactical air support. In these cases, mobile airfields – in the shape of aircraft carriers – provided tactical air support and cover for troops ashore until land-based airfields became operational. This air support had to last anything from two weeks up to two months. It also had to protect the aircraft carriers on which it was based, as well as the invasion's logistical tail, the ships carrying supplies and supporting the troops ashore. This offered another large, tempting target. The strategic heart of any invasion was the aircraft carriers: eliminating those eliminated Allied air superiority.

Three categories of aircraft carriers fought the kamikaze campaign: fleet carriers, light carriers, and escort carriers. Fleet and light carriers were fast vessels built as warships, with a top speed in excess of 30 knots. The major differences between fleet and light carriers were size and capability. Fleet carriers ranged from 25,000–47,000 tons displacement, carried up to 120 aircraft, and had sizable antiaircraft batteries, including 4½in. or 5in. guns. Light carriers displaced between 10,000 and 13,000 tons, carried up to 30 aircraft, and had only light antiaircraft guns. By 1944, these carriers were the heart of every major navy's striking force.

Escort carriers were merchant conversions or purpose-built aircraft carriers based on merchant designs. Roughly the same size as light carriers, they were much slower: most had top speeds of only around 20 knots and cruising speed of 15 knots, while carrying 28–33 aircraft. The US and Royal Navy fielded escort carriers, with most Royal Navy escort carriers built in the US.

Built to mercantile standards, escort carriers lacked the structural integrity and damage control capability of fleet and light carriers. Nevertheless, their greater vulnerability to submarine and aircraft attack was considered acceptable, as they were intended to operate where the Allies possessed air superiority. Escort carrier crews often joked that the US Navy designation for escort carriers – CVE – stood for "combustible, vulnerable, and expendable." This proved sadly true during the kamikaze campaign.

Although some Royal Navy light and escort carriers operated against Japan, most did so in areas removed from kamikaze concentrations. While supporting British Pacific Fleet activities in the Dutch East Indies and Southeast Asia, these ships encountered only occasional kamikaze attack by ad-hoc attackers, not organized *tokkotai*.

A total of 16 United States Navy fleet carriers, nine US light carriers, and five Royal Navy fleet carriers participated in the kamikaze campaign. In addition, around 50 escort carriers played some role in the campaign. If the war had continued until spring 1946 (when Operation *Olympic*, the invasion of Kyushu, was scheduled), another 12 US fleet carriers, one Royal Navy fleet carrier, and up to 50 additional escort carriers could potentially have participated in the overarching *Downfall*.

Two US fleet carriers were prewar vessels: the *Saratoga* and *Enterprise*. USS *Saratoga*, a 47,000 ton giant, was originally intended as a battle cruiser, but was converted to an aircraft carrier during construction. *Enterprise*, sole survivor of the three-ship Yorktown class, displaced 25,000 tons. Both could reach 33 knots and carry in excess of 80 aircraft. The remaining US fleet carriers belonged to the Essex class, some two dozen of which were built. These carriers displaced 35,000 tons loaded, their waterline was 820ft long, they had an 862ft flight deck, had a top speed of 32.5 knots, and could cruise for 20,000nmi at 15 knots. Each Essex-class vessel carried up to 100 aircraft.

All Royal Navy fleet carriers belonged to the Illustrious and Implacable classes. The four Illustrious-class carriers were authorized in 1936, displaced 28,000 tons, had a 30.5 knot top speed, could steam 11,000nmi at 14 knots, and were 675ft long with a 650ft flight deck. Designed to carry 36 aircraft, by 1945 they routinely carried up to 55. The two Implacable-class carriers were improved Illustrious-class ships. At 673ft, they were 2ft shorter at the waterline but had a 750ft flight deck. They had the same range, 11,000nmi at 14 knots, but a top speed of 32 knots. Although designed to carry 54 aircraft, this number rose to 75 during the kamikaze campaign.

The US light carriers all belonged to the Independence class, being conversions modified while under construction from Cleveland-class light cruisers. Each was 600ft long at the waterline, with a 552ft flight deck. They displaced nearly 15,000 tons fully loaded, their steam turbines could reach a top speed of 31 knots, and they could cruise 13,000nmi at 15 knots. Designed to carry 45 aircraft, under combat conditions they carried between 31 and 34.

The US built six different classes of escort carriers, but only two saw significant service during the kamikaze campaign: the Sangamon and Casablanca classes. The Bogue class was primarily used in the Atlantic, while Commencement Bay-class carriers were only completed late in the war: only USS *Block Island* (CVE-106) arrived in time to participate, briefly, in

The Royal Navy and its British Pacific Fleet included four Illustrious-class (shown) and two Implacable-class fleet carriers. While not all were present at one time, generally three or four Royal Navy fleet carriers were present during operations in 1945. (AC)

## OPPOSITE THE PROXIMITY FUZE AND ITS USE

The proximity fuze was a miniature radar in a shell's nose which detonated it at the closest approach to an object, where the shell did the most damage. Its use meant setting shells to explode at a fixed altitude or time, which was almost useless against aircraft rapidly changing altitude or approaching quickly. It allowed direct hits without actually requiring one.

The proximity fuze was one of the key elements leading to the defeat of the kamikazes. This US Navy cutaway shows the interior of the fuze, a miniature radar which fits in the nose of a 5in. antiaircraft shell. (USNHHC)

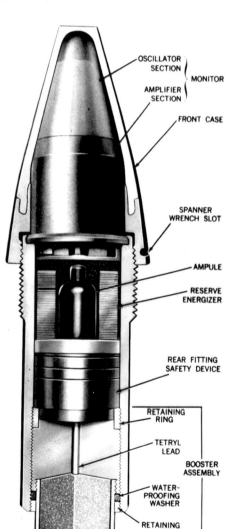

OSCILLATOR SECTION

MONITOR

AMPLIFIER SECTION

FRONT CASE

SPANNER WRENCH SLOT

AMPULE

RESERVE ENERGIZER

REAR FITTING SAFETY DEVICE

RETAINING RING

TETRYL LEAD

BOOSTER ASSEMBLY

WATER-PROOFING WASHER

RETAINING RING

the kamikaze campaign. Both classes would have seen extensive service during *Downfall* if the war had continued.

The four Sangamon-class ships were the largest escort carriers built by the United States, converted from fleet oilers while under construction. They displaced 25,000 tons (as much as the *Enterprise*) and were 525ft long, with a 495ft flight deck. They could make only 18 knots, but could steam 24,000nmi at 15 knots. They carried 30 aircraft.

The Casablanca-class carriers, the smallest at 11,000 tons, were also called the Kaiser carriers, since they were mass-produced at Kaiser Corporation shipyards, built through an initiative of the company's owner, Henry J. Kaiser. They were 490ft long, with a 475ft flight deck, and had a maximum speed of 19 knots. They steamed 10,200nmi at 15 knots and carried 28 aircraft. Fifty Casablanca carriers were built. Five served in the Atlantic, while the rest went to the Pacific. However, not all 45 of these saw combat, as some were used for carrier training or as aircraft transports.

All US carriers had wooden flight decks to reduce weight aloft and increase aircraft capacity. British fleet carriers, however, had armored flight decks, one reason they carried fewer aircraft than their US Navy counterparts. Although the disadvantage of wooden flight decks and advantages of armored flight decks were known through combat experience prior to the kamikaze campaign, US Navy naval architects knew a bomb dropped by a dive bomber hit with enough energy to penetrate even an armored flight deck. An armored flight deck thus offered no more meaningful protection than a wooden deck. Furthermore, when naval treaties had limited warships' weight, the extra protection offered by an armored flight deck failed to offset its weight penalty.

Yet a kamikaze aircraft lacked the penetrating power of an armor-piercing bomb: it smashed through a wooden flight deck, but bounced off an armored one. An anonymous US Navy liaison officer aboard HMS *Indefatigable* summed up the difference in a report where he stated, "When a kamikaze hits a US carrier, it's six months repair at Pearl. In a Limey carrier it's a case of 'sweepers, man your brooms.'"

## Weapons and tactics

The Allies used a variety of weapons and tactics to combat kamikazes. Some existed prior to the launch of kamikaze attacks, while others – especially tactics – were developed to meet the new threat.

All US-built aircraft, including those used by the Royal Navy's Fleet Air Arm, carried the M2 Browning .50cal machine gun. Seafires were armed with two Hispano-Suiza HS.404 Mk II 20mm cannon and four .303 Browning machine guns. These were the primary weapons used by Allied aircraft against kamikazes and the Japanese aircraft supporting them.

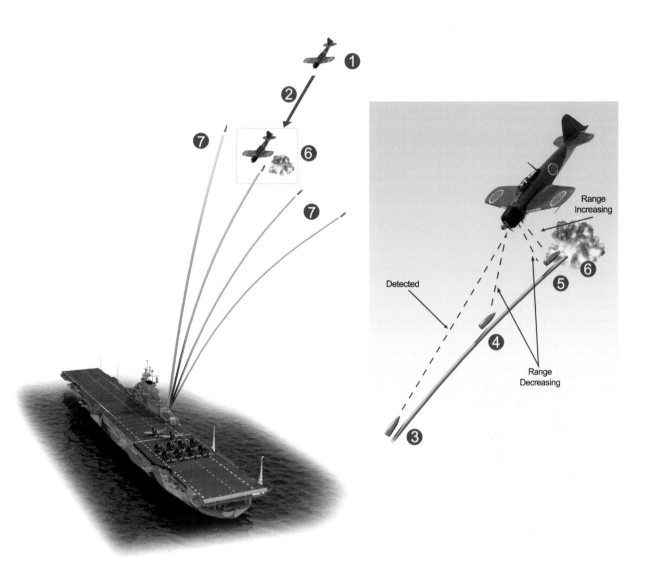

## EVENTS

1. Kamikaze begins dive on US Navy aircraft carrier.

2. Using radar guidance, the carrier engages with its 5in battery, firing a spread of shells to ensure one comes close enough.

3. Proximity-fuzed shell detects object with its radar.

4. While range decreases, shell does not explode.

5. Shell reaches point of closest approach, range still decreasing.

6. As shell passes point of closest approach, range increases and fuze detonates shell.

7. Other shells continue until their radar spots a target or they detonate at end of run.

The Mark 14 gunsight automatically calculated the "lead" required to hit a fast-moving target. This drawing, taken from a World War II US Navy training manual, explained to gun crews how to use the sight. (AC)

The M2 .50cal was an air-cooled and highly reliable machine gun, with naval aircraft using a dedicated aircraft version, the AN/M2. The M2 had a muzzle velocity of 2,910ft/s and could fire 750–850 rounds per minute. The gun fired a 52g bullet, capable of penetrating 1in. of armor and structural steel of unarmored ships. It was potent against ships, ground vehicles, and buildings as well as other aircraft.

The .303 Browning was a British and smaller version of the Browning .50cal, with an 11g round and a muzzle-velocity of 2,800ft/s. Aircraft versions fired 1,200–1,500 rounds per minute. The 20mm Mk II autocannon fired a .25kg round, and with a muzzle velocity of 870m/s it could fire 650–700 rounds per minute.

Allied warships were protected by a variety of antiaircraft artillery. The heaviest antiaircraft protection for US Navy ships was provided by 5in./38cal guns. On Royal Navy ships, the 5¼in., 4½in., and 4in. guns served this purpose. These were backed up by an array of 40mm Bofors and 20mm Oerlikon antiaircraft guns mounted on both nations' warships.

The 5in./38cal gun was the finest dual-purpose naval gun of World War II, effective and deadly against aircraft, especially when accurate aircraft altitudes were provided for fuzing or when proximity fuzes were fitted. The shell weighed 55lb, of which 7–8½lb was the bursting charge. The gun fired 15 rounds per minute, had a 37, 200ft ceiling, and could reach low-flying aircraft up to 13½ nautical miles away.

The 5¼in. Mk I gun used aboard British battleships and antiaircraft cruisers fired an 80lb round. It had a muzzle velocity of 2,672ft/s, a 36,000ft ceiling, an effective range of 11nmi, and fired eight rounds per minute. The 4½in./45cal gun used aboard British aircraft carriers and late-war destroyers fired a 31lb projectile. It had a muzzle velocity of 2,350ft/s, a 29,910ft ceiling, an effective range of 9.8nmi, and fired 12 rounds per minute. The 4in. gun used aboard cruisers fired a 55lb projectile. It had a muzzle velocity of 2,387ft/s, a 28,750ft ceiling, an effective range of just over 6½nmi, and could fire between nine and 14 rounds per minute.

The 40mm gun was a Swedish Bofors design, built under license in the United States. It fired a 2lb explosive round, could fire 120 rounds per minute, and had a 22,300ft ceiling. To minimize the danger of friendly-fire, rounds were typically fuzed to explode after traveling 12,000–15,000ft, within which distance they were deadly.

The 20mm gun, a Swiss Oerlikon design produced under license, fired a ¼lb projectile. Its effective rate of fire was 250–320 rounds per minute. It had a 10,000ft ceiling, although it was rarely effective beyond 3,000ft. US Navy doctrine was to begin firing 20mm guns when the target was 3,900ft away, allowing aimed corrections as the target entered effective range.

Antiaircraft defense started with radar, which vectored Allied aircraft towards attacking Japanese aircraft and controlled fire once enemy planes arrived within range of shipboard artillery. By October 1944, every major Allied warship had radar. Most large warships had some version of SK air search radar, which had a range of 162nmi if the aircraft was in line of sight. Destroyer escorts were normally equipped with SA air search radar, although some had SK radar.

Additionally, by 1944, destroyers and larger warships had fire-control radar to provide both the azimuth and altitude of incoming aircraft.

One of the tools most responsible for neutralizing the kamikaze threat, yet least appreciated for the role it played, was the fog nozzle. It significantly improved firefighting efforts aboard Allied warships, neutralizing the kamikaze's greatest threat: fire. (AC)

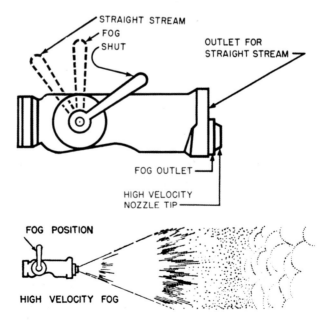

STRAIGHT STREAM
FOG
SHUT
OUTLET FOR STRAIGHT STREAM
FOG OUTLET
HIGH VELOCITY NOZZLE TIP
FOG POSITION
HIGH VELOCITY FOG

This directed the fire of the 5in./38cal antiaircraft guns that formed destroyers' main batteries and the secondary batteries of cruisers, aircraft carriers, and battleships. This was particularly effective when the directed guns used proximity fuzes.

The proximity fuze used a radar unit inside the projectile. If the radar detected an object (hopefully an enemy aircraft), it detonated the shell just after the closest approach, when the range began increasing. This dramatically increased the odds of the shell exploding within the fatal burst radius of an aircraft.

While proximity fuzes could not be fitted in 40mm and 20mm shells, their volume of fire mitigated this disadvantage. The 40mm guns used the Mark 37 director, which was originally an optical system but by late 1944 was radar-equipped. Later, a Mark 51 director was developed, optimized for a 40mm gun. The 40mm and 20mm guns could also be directed locally using the Mark 14 gunsight, which used gyroscopes to calculate how much to "lead" a moving target. Most of these innovations were pioneered by Charles Stark Draper in the Massachusetts Institute of Technology MIT Instrumentation Laboratory. Between October 1944 and August 1945, 80 percent of all Japanese aircraft shot down were engaged by Draper-equipped antiaircraft guns.

Damage control has been underappreciated by many naval historians. By late 1944, Allied navies had achieved remarkable competence in containing and controlling battle damage. This was especially true for firefighting, as wartime experience revealed fire as the biggest combat risk to ships, especially aircraft carriers that were filled with explosives and volatile aircraft fuel. The US Navy increased the number of fire mains aboard ships. It installed fire mains powered independently of ships' engines or added portable, gasoline-powered water pumps. Aircraft carriers also carried foaming systems to quench fuel fires.

The most important improvement was the fog nozzle. Water quenches fire primarily by depriving it of heat. The fog nozzle sprayed water in a fine mist, maximizing the exposed surface area. Whereas a solid stream of water scattered flammable aviation gasoline, thereby spreading the fire, fogged mist did not do this.

The Allies developed dedicated tactics to counter kamikazes. The three most important were radar picket destroyers, "delousing," and the "Big Blue Blanket." On strike days, destroyers were placed on either side of the axis of attack, 60 miles closer to the enemy than the carriers. They were equipped with air search radar and aircraft homing beacons. Combat Air Patrols (CAP) were maintained over these "Tom Cat" picket destroyers to deal with enemy aircraft.

Friendly aircraft returning from missions flew over Tom Cat destroyers, doing a full 360-degree turn over them. The returning strike then flew to the carriers, tracing a dogleg course. The CAP "deloused" the aircraft over the Tom Cats, identifying friendly and enemy aircraft, attacking any hostile planes attempting to sneak in with the returning strike. Any aircraft skipping the Tom Cats, flying a straight course to the carriers, were assumed to be hostile and intercepted by the carrier group's CAP.

The Big Blue Blanket smothered any attempt to mount a kamikaze attack by closing all airfields available to them. Fighter groups were sent to every airfield within range of the carrier group, with patrols placed over each airfield. Any Japanese aircraft attempting to take off were shot down. As aircraft grew low on fuel, patrols were relieved by new fighter groups. Bomber strikes attacked any aircraft on the ground during this changing of the guard. The umbrella blanketed these airfields round-the-clock, sometimes for days.

These tactics required more fighters, so fleet carriers increased the fighters carried from 36 to 73, cutting the dive bombers and torpedo bombers to 15 each from 36 and 18 respectively. Another change involved reducing the number of carrier groups from four to three. Increasing the number of ships in each group beefed up antiaircraft defenses, while reducing the number of groups eased the number of fighters required for CAP by one-third.

# CAMPAIGN OBJECTIVES
## The last throw of the dice

Initial Japanese success in the Pacific War had been reversed by late 1943, when Japan's air forces lost their superiority over Allied aircraft. Between January and December 1943, Allied air forces gained superiority in aircraft quality and quantity. As the year ended, Japanese aerial forces were on the defensive everywhere.

Frontline Allied fighters – the Hellcats, Corsairs, and USAAF P-38 Lightnings and P-47 Thunderbolts – outclassed even the latest Japanese fighters. Meanwhile, four-engine B-17 and B-24 bombers were strongly built with heavy defensive armament. Weapons carried by Japanese fighters – generally only a pair of machine guns – were too weak to shoot them down in one pass. Attacking them often ended in the attacker's destruction. Similarly, Allied warships possessed powerful antiaircraft batteries, which frequently shot down attacking aircraft. The Allies captured the Marianas islands during the middle of 1944. After the destruction of the last credible Japanese carrier force during that campaign, there seemed little to stop the Allies bearing down on Japan. Frontline Japanese aviators began concluding that orthodox tactics against Allied aircraft and ships were futile. No new weapons, aircraft, or miracle defensive techniques seemed available; only suicide tactics promised success. Individual Japanese pilots, deciding they were doomed anyway, chose to "take one with them," deliberately ramming aircraft or crashing into ships.

These attacks were initially ad hoc, spur-of-the-moment decisions by individual pilots, but as time passed and Japanese desperation grew, more pilots participated in such attacks. Eventually, realization grew among pilots willing to make suicide attacks that they would be most effective if coordinated. This clamor led one Japanese admiral to experiment by organizing one such unit among volunteers in his command. Initial success in the Philippines led to its growth, and it became a policy endorsed by the Japanese High Command. Once in place, the kamikaze campaign rapidly expanded.

The campaign required a reaction by the Allies. Their first difficulty was recognizing the problem. They knew that the Japanese were fanatical opponents who routinely fought even when the odds of victory were impossible, but it took longer to recognize that the enemy

A painting by a Japanese artist of kamikaze pilots at an airfield in Kyushu, awaiting an upcoming mission against Allied forces in Okinawa. (AC)

would deliberately make suicide attacks. Nevertheless, within a week of the first such attacks, made during the battle of Leyte Gulf in October 1944, the Allies were developing defenses against kamikazes.

At first, as with the Japanese, the responses were ad hoc, and developed from the bottom up. Soon, however, comprehensive plans were being developed and executed to counter the kamikaze threat. The US Navy, bearing the brunt of the kamikaze campaign, set its best tactical thinkers to develop countermeasures. These were adopted as part of an integrated overall plan executed by the entire Allied fleet closing in on Japan.

The result was a campaign where the Japanese attackers pursued a defensive strategic objective while the Allies were on the tactical defensive while pursuing an offensive strategic objective. It was an improvised campaign, on both sides, with fixed strategic objectives and constantly shifting tactical plans.

## Japanese objectives and plans

Japan initiated the kamikaze campaign with one strategic objective: to prevent an Allied invasion of Japan. The belief was that if enough Allied ships were sunk, invasion would be impossible. Failing that, the campaign was intended to increase Allied casualties to an unacceptably high level, which it was believed would lead the Allies to a negotiated peace.

However, the Japanese realized either outcome was unlikely. Yet the alternative, the unconditional surrender demanded by the Allies, was unthinkable in a nation led by the world's last god-king. Japan needed to end the war, but knew it could no longer win the

The first coordinated US Navy responses to the kamikaze threat were developed by Commander John Thatch (foreground), TF38's operations officer, and its commander, Vice Admiral John McCain (background). Their tactics proved effective countermeasures against kamikazes. (USNHHC)

war in any meaningful sense. Survival of the state, defined as the survival of Imperial Japan, was now considered to be a victory. Although the kamikaze campaign offered little chance of success and had to be conducted at an unreasonable cost, it seemed the only path to ending the war on Imperial Japan's terms. But Japan entered the campaign reluctantly. As with much of Japanese war policy, it did not emerge from the Japanese High Command: it was forced upon them by subordinates, including those participating as kamikazes.

In July 1944, the Imperial Japanese Army began investigating the use of *tokko* units, drawing up plans to create them but stopping short of actually creating them. Organizational, training, and tactical plans were complete by August. Volunteers to man these special attack units were sought from Army flight training schools, and 60 were recruited by the end of September. The Army also began converting twin-engine Ki-48 and Ki-67 bombers into suicide aircraft.

Meanwhile, the Imperial Japanese Navy was also considering *tokko* units. Following the battle of the Philippine Sea on June 19 and 20, 1944, Rear Admiral Obayashi Sueo, commanding the IJN's Third Carrier Division, offered to organize special attack units. He took the proposal to Vice Admiral Ozawa Jisaburō, commanding the Mobile Fleet. Ozawa informed Admiral Soemu Toyoda, the Commander-in-Chief of the IJN, but no action was taken. Ozawa believed that special attacks had to be voluntary, and felt organizing *tokko* units would undermine their voluntary nature.

Vice Admiral Ōnishi Takijirō was initially opposed to *tokko* tactics, but reversed his position when he inherited command of Japanese Naval Air Forces in the Philippines. He authorized the first set of kamikaze attacks. (AC)

In September 1944, the Army and Navy began studies on how to prevent future Allied invasions and stop invasion fleets. The studies concluded that IJA and IJN pilots lacked the skill to conduct effective high-level attacks against ships. Moreover, training was required for effective mast-top and skip bombing, training that would consume scarce stores of fuel and supplies. The effectiveness of Allied antiaircraft defenses meant mast-top bombing would generate prohibitive losses. The only effective tactic remaining seemed to be crashing aircraft into the target, which promised sufficient accuracy and would neutralize much of the Allied antiaircraft advantages as a fatally hit aircraft could still reach its target.

Despite this, by September, the Japanese were unwilling to actually organize *tokko* units. They had the plans and resources in place, should they decide to activate them, but even into late October the Imperial General Headquarters was not ready to commit to *tokko* units or tactics.

Even so, local commanders were pushing ahead. The Fourth Air Army in the Philippines began forming *tokko* units in September 1944, committing three Nakajima Ki-43 Hayabusas in *tokko* attacks against Task Force 58 when it raided Luzon. Rear Admiral Arima Masabumi, Commander of the 26th Air Flotilla in the Philippines, also decided to create *tokko* units. He died piloting a Yokosuka D4Y1 against the US fleet carrier *Franklin* on October 15, and was hailed in Japan as the first kamikaze. Whether this was intended as a suicide attack remains controversial. Whatever the truth, a CAP shot Arima down before he reached the *Franklin*.

Vice Admiral Ōnishi Takijirō replaced Arima two days later, taking charge of the IJN's First Air Fleet in October 1944. This naval air fleet held responsibility for defending the

Northern Philippines, and Ōnishi inherited Arima's *tokko* unit. Although previously opposed to *tokko* tactics, Ōnishi reversed his position, feeling he lacked the strength to defeat an Allied invasion using conventional tactics.

This force was christened the Kamikaze Special Attack Unit, invoking memories of the Divine Wind typhoon which scattered Kublai Khan's invasion fleet in AD 1280. The unit's name was subsequently applied to all IJN special attack groups. (The Allies adopted kamikaze as a generic description of suicide units and personnel, probably to the IJA's discontent.) These units saw action during the battle of Leyte Gulf, most successfully on October 25, when returning Japanese escort fighters reported four kamikazes successfully hit their targets, sinking three fleet carriers. In reality, they sank just one escort carrier but damaged five others.

However, reality mattered less than perception. The First Kamikaze Special Attack Group, intended as a one-off effort, apparently yielded impressive results, being credited with 28 hits scored from the 60 kamikazes expended, a nearly 50 percent success rate. This compared favorably to conventional attacks by the Second Air Fleet when it was committed to the battle for Leyte. The latter were so unsuccessful that the Second Air Fleet subsequently formed its own kamikaze corps, apparently obtaining 19 successful strikes with 70 kamikazes.

Thereafter, the Imperial General Headquarters blessed the kamikaze concept, and both the Army and Navy high commands activated previously developed plans for deploying kamikazes. In reality, they were simply trying to catch up to the commanders in the field, rather than asserting their authority.

Their efforts included planning and implementing production of dedicated suicide aircraft. The best-known examples were the Ohka rocket-bomb and the Ki-115 Tsurugi. Massive production was planned for both aircraft, including up to 8,000 Ki-115s, but actual production fell far short of goals: nearly 900 Ohkas and just 105 Ki-115s.

The Ki-115 was built as a kamikaze aircraft, with landing gear that could be jettisoned and no armament save for a bomb. Production of 8,000 was ordered, although only 115 had been completed by the war's end. (SDFM)

Once unleashed, the kamikaze campaign could not be constrained, only steered. The sacrifices made by previous kamikazes impelled others to match them. Even the emperor, theoretically the head of Japan's armed forces, could not stop it. When briefed on the Philippine special attacks, he responded with, "Was it necessary to go to this extreme? They certainly did a magnificent job!" Japan's military leaders focused on the emperor's second sentence rather than the first. Ignoring his reluctance to employ suicide tactics, they used his praise for the kamikazes' sacrifices as imperial endorsement of *tokko*.

The IJA joined the kamikaze campaign in November. Unlike the Navy, the Army's first kamikaze aircraft and volunteers came largely from their Philippines-based training schools, but little formal planning was apparent in their initial deployment. The aircraft carefully converted during July, August, and September were committed, but once expended do not appear to have been replaced with new conversions. Instead, conventional aircraft were used throughout the rest of the campaign.

Doctrine for both services used kamikazes as a reactive tool. With few exceptions, they were deployed where the Allies were expected to strike, collected in advance near locations thought likely to be the site of Allied landings. When the Allies cooperated with Japanese plans, they were met almost immediately by kamikazes. However, the Allies' habit of striking at unexpected places and unexpected times also forced Japan to scramble around redeploying kamikazes to counter the threat.

Sometimes, as in carrier strikes in the South China Sea or against Japan, kamikazes appeared only as Allied carriers were returning to base, wasting gasoline and putting wear on aircraft without any positive effect. At other times, such as the invasions of Iwo Jima and Okinawa, the kamikazes arrived in force only after ground troops were firmly ashore, which deprived kamikazes of fully laden troopships as targets. Additionally, the Allies confounded Japanese pre-positional planning by neutralizing potential kamikaze airfields prior to invading.

The IJA and IJN did not initially coordinate planning, with the services tending to focus on different objectives. The Navy wanted to destroy the enemy's carriers, believing the Allies would not invade without air support, whereas the Army concentrated on destroying transports carrying invasion troops, believing that reducing the ground forces which landed improved the defenders' chances of victory. This lack of coordination diluted efforts, even within individual phases of the campaign.

This was rectified after the Iwo Jima campaign. The next obvious objective was the Ryukyus, as these islands provided airfields within range of Kyushu, the southernmost of Japan's four major Home Islands. A coordinated plan was thus developed to defend it. For the first time in the Pacific War, a unified Japanese air command was established. All aircraft in Kyushu – Army and Navy – were placed under command of the the IJN's air force. Tactical command was assigned to Vice Admiral Ugaki Matome, who assigned targets for all aircraft, although each service planned the tactics used by their aircraft. Formosa retained the kamikaze aircraft assigned to it, with the understanding they were to be used to mount attacks against the Ryukyus once the Allies invaded. Consequently, the Allies experienced the first coordinated kamikaze effort of the campaign.

Preparations for the final defense of the Japanese homeland were even more rigorous. By the summer of 1945, planning for a kamikaze defense of Japan was well underway, with emphasis placed on holding Kyushu. Between one-third and three-quarters of all available kamikaze aircraft in Japan (estimated at 5,000 by postwar US analysis) would have been committed to stopping Operation *Olympic*, the Allied invasion scheduled for November 1, 1945.

## Allied objectives and plans

The Allied grand strategic objective in the Pacific War was the unconditional surrender of the Empire of Japan. As the Japanese kamikaze campaign threatened the achievement of that objective, the Allies realized they had to neutralize or minimize the kamikaze threat.

It took time for the Allies to realize a problem existed. The first kamikaze attacks were extemporaneous efforts on September 13, 1944, by three IJA Ki-43s which went unrecognized as suicidal attacks. The Hayabusas were either shot down before they could hit a ship or the Allies assumed a mortally wounded pilot had deliberately crashed into a vessel. The latter act, routinely attempted by the Japanese throughout the Pacific War, was viewed as different from deliberately setting out to crash undamaged aircraft into vessels.

US signal intelligence may have picked up chatter about suicide tactics between July and October 1944, when the Japanese first considered it. If so, it was either dismissed as speculation or not worth potentially compromising the secret that the US was reading Japan's radio messages. Regardless, it was not until the October 25, 1944, attacks on Task Group 77.4 that the new Japanese attack tactics were recognized. It took another week for the US and its allies to realize this would be an ongoing problem.

Due to their commitment to support the landings at Leyte, there was little the US Navy could do by way of planning or operational changes until the end of November. The Fast Carrier Task Force had to remain at sea flying combat missions. Only minor adjustments could be made, such as increasing CAP duration and the number of fighters assigned to combat air patrols. Once the fleet returned to its Ulithi anchorage in the Caroline Islands, the problem was tackled.

The US Navy maintained two fleets in the Pacific – the Third Fleet and the Fifth Fleet. Both operated the same ships and used the same structure. Regardless of which fleet, these ships were called the "Big Blue Fleet." When the fleets "changed," the commanders and command staff changed and the lead number in each task force switched. Task Force 38, the fast carrier force, went from TF38 (Task Force 38) to TF58 or vice versa. The Third Fleet was commanded by Admiral William Halsey, the Fifth Fleet by Admiral Raymond Spruance.

While Halsey commanded the Third Fleet, Spruance and his staff planned operations for the next major offensive. When Spruance took over, the Third Fleet became the Fifth Fleet, and Halsey and his staff began planning for the next offensive. The system was first implemented with the Marianas campaign in April 1944, when the Fifth Fleet was activated. It rotated back to being the Third Fleet in September, for the Peleliu and Philippines operations, before Spruance took over again in February 1945 for the invasion of Iwo Jima and the Bonin Islands.

In the meantime, operational responsibility for the fast carriers was in the hands of Halsey's Fast Carrier Task Force Commander, Vice Admiral John S. McCain. Short in stature and nicknamed "Slew," McCain gained his aviator wings in 1936, one of the oldest men to become a naval flyer. He was Commander, Aircraft, South Pacific, during the Guadalcanal campaign. He gained command of the Third Fleet's TF38 on October 30, 1944, when the Fast Carrier Task Force's previous commander, Admiral Marc Mitscher, was assigned to command TF58 exclusively.

McCain had two talented tacticians on his staff. His chief of staff was Rear Admiral Wilder D. Baker, a submariner who became an operation research expert earlier in the war, and his operations officer was John "Jimmy" S. Thatch, a tactical mastermind who invented the "Thatch Weave," which allowed the inferior Wildcat to meet Zeros on equal terms.

The three got together to counter the kamikaze threat, and quickly developed several important tactics. The first and most vital

Vice Admiral Ugaki Matome was given overall command of all *tokko* forces in Kyushu early in 1945. He coordinated kamikaze attacks in Okinawa and planned the kamikaze response for the expected invasion of Kyushu. (AC)

involved changing the organization of TF38 and the aircraft carried by the fleet carriers. At Leyte, TF38 was broken into four carrier task groups, each with four or five fast carriers. In December, it was changed to three task groups. Additionally, the ratio of fighters to bombers was changed; instead of a roughly even split between fighters, dive bombers, and torpedo bombers on each fleet carrier, fighters were increased to two-thirds of the aircraft complement.

Reducing the number of carrier groups limited the tactical flexibility offered by four independent carrier groups. This was offset by two things: it increased the antiaircraft firepower and CAP aircraft available to each task group by increasing the number of escorting ships and aircraft carriers, and reduced the number of task groups to defend. Ultimately, tactical flexibility was viewed as more important. Mitscher, when TF38 became TF58, reverted to the four carrier task group structure.

The US Navy increased light and medium antiaircraft provision throughout World War II, such as the quad 40mm guns pictured. By autumn 1944, a US Navy task group could saturate the sky with 40mm and 20mm antiaircraft fire. (AC)

The increased fighter complement became permanent, however. Ironically, a change implemented as a defensive measure increased the carriers' offensive potential. Hellcats and Corsairs carried almost as big a bombload as the Navy bombers, but were faster and could serve as fighters after dropping their ordnance. Except against heavily armored aircraft carriers, battleships, and heavy cruisers, mast-top bombing was more effective against ships than dive bombing, but few Japanese heavy warships offered themselves as targets after the battle of Leyte Gulf. Hellcats and Corsairs were better at mast-top attacks, with the fighters' multiple forward-firing machine guns, which bombers lacked, suppressing Japanese antiaircraft fire during the approach.

Some changes applied only to fleet carriers, with light carriers and escort carriers maintaining the same ratio of fighters to bombers as before. The light carriers operated within the Fast Carrier Task Force, while escort carriers provided tactical support for invasion troops or served as aircraft ferries.

The escort carriers with replacement aircraft for the Fast Carrier Task Force operated as part of TG30.8 or TG50.8 (depending on the active fleet), while those assigned to invasion support were part of the Seventh Fleet in TG77.4. While tactical support escort carriers were broken into three task units during Leyte, they operated in two during subsequent invasions, with more carriers in each unit. Although the Fast Carrier Task Force provided overall CAP in a theater, the escort carrier groups were also responsible for their local protection. They emulated the fast carrier force in using delousing tactics and providing local CAP over their units. However, they primarily had less-capable Wildcats for fighter cover, offering kamikazes better opportunities when attacking escort carrier groups.

The most important innovation developed by Thatch was the "Big Blue Blanket." Like dropping a blanket over a fire to smother it, the Big Blue Blanket "smothered" kamikazes. Kamikazes posed no threat if they could not take off. This was done by stationing dawn-to-dusk Allied air cover over all airfields potentially available to kamikaze aircraft during an invasion's opening phase, protecting an invasion force (typically the Seventh Fleet) throughout a critical period. It required a great deal of planning and coordination to execute, but it proved effective, even against targets as large as Luzon.

This strategy was first implemented in advance of the Mindoro and Lingayen Bay landings in the Philippines in December and January 1944. It also successfully shut down enemy airfields in the Bonins and Ryukyus during the opening phases of the Iwo Jima and Okinawa invasions. Its utility was limited when distant bases permitted kamikazes to reach the invasion fleet, Formosa serving this role during the Lingayen Bay and Okinawa landings, as did the Japanese Home Islands during operations at Iwo Jima and Okinawa.

Radar pickets countered this tactic of kamikazes flying from distant bases. These differed from Tom Cat pickets in intent and disposition. Tom Cats identified friendly aircraft returning to their carrier, and separated out and eliminated kamikazes attempting to sneak in with the friendlies. Radar pickets, however, provided early warning of kamikazes approaching from distant airfields.

Radar pickets were first used at Okinawa after the experience at Iwo Jima, where the Japanese launched surprise kamikaze raids from the Home Islands, refueling at intermediate and otherwise unoccupied airfields distant from Iwo Jima. To prevent similar surprises at Okinawa, radar pickets were stationed between Kyushu and Okinawa, each picket consisting of a destroyer or a destroyer escort supported by LCS(L)s.

Radar pickets maintained a continuous radar and visual air search of approaches taken by Japanese aircraft. Contacts were reported to the fleet's Officer-in-Tactical Command (OTC) of air defense and fighters airborne at a ready reaction point (called point BOLO at Okinawa). Fighters were dispatched to intercept the bogies (slang for hostile aircraft), with the radar picket then serving as a fighter director for the interceptors.

Shutting down Japanese airfields was another key to containing the kamikaze threat, as kamikazes could not attack if they could not get airborne. This airfield on Okinawa is being bombed by carrier aircraft in one such effort. (AC)

This provided defense in depth for the invasion by Seventh Fleet and the covering Third Fleet, allowing an extra hour's warning of kamikaze attacks. It also tended to divert kamikazes from the major fleets, as many kamikazes attacked the first ship they saw, which were most frequently the picket ships. It was hard on the radar pickets, but destroyers, destroyer escorts, and LSC(L)s were more numerous and far more expendable than fast carriers or loaded troop transports.

# THE CAMPAIGN
## Dying for the Emperor

Self-sacrifice is part of warfare, closely linked to heroism. US soldiers joke that the surest way of winning the Medal of Honor, the nation's highest reward for heroism, is to throw yourself on a live grenade to save your buddies. The almost certainty of individual death is measured against the lives saved by that sacrifice. Nor is fighting to the death unknown in Western culture: the Alamo and Custer's Last Stand are honored in the United States, while in Europe, events as remote at the battle of Roncevaux Pass and as recent as the 1943 Warsaw Ghetto uprising are remembered.

The kamikaze campaign was different. The entire campaign was an exercise in deliberate, mass suicide. No other air campaign was fought under those conditions. However, it was unique among the Japanese Pacific War effort only in its scale. For whereas an Allied soldier might fall on a live grenade to save his buddies, Japanese troops would hold one next to their bodies to avoid the shame of surrender.

The last stands of Western culture were fought when surrender was impossible or when a fight to the death was necessary to delay the enemy for strategic reasons. The Jews of the Warsaw Ghetto fought because they knew the Nazis were going to kill them anyway, so they decided to take as many Nazis as possible with them before they died. In Japan during the Pacific War, when defeat seemed inevitable, soldiers frequently threw themselves on the enemy in a suicidal attack, known to GIs and Marines as a Banzai charge. The primary purpose of the attack was to obtain an honorable death. Enemy casualties, while a desirable byproduct, were secondary.

The roots of this belief lay in Japanese culture and society, especially its religion. Imperial Japan's emperor was its supreme deity, the highest in a vast pantheon. The Japanese Bushido, the military code of its feudal warriors, meant there was no higher honor than to die for the emperor. There was no greater disgrace than to disappoint the emperor through surrender.

This belief was carefully cultivated by the military dictatorship which took control of Japan in the 1920s. In 1931, outside Shanghai, three Japanese soldiers carrying a

No side had a monopoly on courage or the willingness to sacrifice one's own life when called for. US Navy sailors frequently took near-suicidal risks battling fires aboard their ships, especially when necessary to save shipmates. (AC)

Japanese kamikaze pilots prepare for battle somewhere in the Philippines. A comrade tightens a *hachimaki*, a folded cloth to keep perspiration from the eyes, for a kamikaze pilot ready to sortie. The *hachimaki* symbolized the manly composure of kamikaze pilots. (USNHHC)

breaching charge through barbed wire defences deliberately blew the charge while next to it to ensure a breach was effected. A statue was raised to the men, who were hailed as examples to be emulated. They, and all those who died in military service for the emperor, were enshrined at Yasukuni Shrine in Tokyo as *kami* (deities). To die for the emperor was to gain divinity.

This belief was the basis of the kamikaze campaign and fueled the kamikaze spirit. Lieutenant General Kawabe, commander of the IJA's air general headquarters, stated after the war: "Everyone who participated in these attacks died happily in the conviction that he would win the final victory by his own death. The Japanese … believed that by spiritual means they could fight on equal terms with you, yet by any other comparison it would not appear equal. We believed our spiritual conviction in victory would balance any scientific advantage [held by the Allies]."

He added:

You call our Kamikaze attacks "suicide attacks." This is a misnomer, and we felt very badly about your calling them "suicide" attacks. They were in no sense "suicide." The pilot did not start out on his mission with the intention of committing suicide. He looked upon himself as a human bomb which would destroy a certain part of the enemy fleet for his country. They considered it a glorious thing, while a "suicide" may not be so glorious.

The early kamikazes were all volunteers, filled with this attitude. Even after this pool of men was exhausted, and Japan resorted to conscripting "volunteers" into *tokko* units, most of those so selected still willingly participated. One such volunteer, saved from death by surrender, stated afterwards that he was "saddened to tears at receiving the death sentence [although] it is unmanly to say so."

This was the context in which Japan started the kamikaze campaign. The result was a no-holds-barred fight, with literally no quarter asked for or received by either the Japanese or Allies. It began when activated by the Allied invasion of the Philippines in October 1944 and reached a climax during the ten-week struggle for Okinawa, but continued until the war ended in August 1945. Even the war's end brought a spate of kamikaze attacks by volunteers unwilling to accept their emperor's command to lay down their arms.

# The first round: October 25–November 30, 1944

The kamikaze campaign opened quietly. On October 19, 1944, Vice Admiral Ōnishi Takijirō, commanding the First Air Fleet in the Philippines, activated the Kamikaze Special Attack Corps, in response to Japan activating *Sho-Go*. The IJN's planned response to an anticipated Allied invasion of the Philippines, *Sho-Go* was activated the previous day after intelligence indicated Allied fleets were moving towards the Philippines.

The Kamikaze Special Attack Corps was organized from 24 volunteer pilots from the Navy's 201st (Fighter) Group, stationed near Manila. The pilots were organized into four units, each with six pilots, and were assigned converted Zeros. Thriftily, the Japanese stripped these aircraft of radio, guns, and all but essential flight instruments, and armed each with a single 250kg bomb. The force was then dispersed, with some units sent to bases in Cebu and Davao in Mindanao. The rest operated out of Mabalacat, a satellite of Clark Field.

Pilots were instructed to execute crash attacks only against major Allied warships. Aircraft carriers had priority, while battleships were also acceptable. Smaller ships, however, were to be ignored. By Ōnishi's calculation, 24 kamikazes were sufficient against the US Fast Carrier Task Force, estimated at between 12 and 20 fast carriers. Without the fast carriers, the Allies would be forced to withdraw their invasion force. Diluting the attacks by hitting minor warships meant too few kamikazes would remain to sufficiently cripple the fast carriers.

When the kamikaze sorties began on October 21, the initial attacks were ineffective. An unexpected strike by US carrier aircraft destroyed the entire six-plane unit on Cebu. The kamikaze pilots used three unmodified Zeros, the only surviving aircraft at the base, to conduct the mission regardless. Two of these were forced to return to base, weather preventing them from finding the Allied fleet. The third aircraft did find the fleet and launched its attack.

It apparently crashed into HMAS *Australia*, a heavy cruiser operating with the US Seventh Fleet, supporting the upcoming Leyte invasion. It was the first successful kamikaze attack and the first of four times *Australia* would be hit by kamikazes. Ironically, the attack went unrecognized as a kamikaze strike as it occurred intermixed with conventional bombing attacks on TF77, the Seventh Fleet's battle force. Allied commanders debated whether the crash was deliberate, but most concluded it was either accidental or spontaneous.

The First Kamikaze Special Attack Group flew additional missions on October 22 and 23 with three of the group's four units. However, these were unsuccessful. Either the searches failed to find enemy warships or the attacks could not be made. The aircraft returned to base, their pilots hoping for better opportunities later.

That opportunity occurred just two days afterwards, on October 25, when the battle of Leyte Gulf was in full swing. TF77, attacked by the *Yamato* unit out of Cebu on October 21, demolished a Japanese surface force in the battle of Surigao Strait, fought during the pre-dawn hours of October 25. TF38 was chasing after the IJN's carrier force, north of Luzon. The carriers were empty of aircraft, being used as bait, intended to lure the Allied fast carriers away from Leyte Gulf. Meanwhile, the Japanese Main Body was exiting the San Bernardino Strait north of Samar, intent on a rendezvous with TF78 and TF79, the invasion support ships stationed off Leyte.

The Main Body instead encountered Task Unit 3 of TF77.4 exiting San Bernardino Strait. Known by its radio call sign, Taffy 3, it was one of three escort carrier units providing air support for the Leyte invasion. It had already launched dawn strikes at the beachhead when the Main Body, commanded by Admiral Kurita Takeo, appeared. Kurita assumed he had found part of the Fast Carrier Task Force, and attacked Taffy 3.

It was an unequal fight, with Japanese battleships and cruisers against a US force comprised of escort carriers, screened by destroyers and destroyer escorts. The screen attacked the Japanese battleships to buy time for the escort carriers to escape. A wild melee ensued, Kurita exchanging the loss of three heavy cruisers for the escort carrier USS *Gambier Bay*, two destroyers, and a destroyer escort before withdrawing back to the San Bernardino Strait and ultimately Japan.

This set the stage for the appearance of the First Kamikaze Group. The first recipients of their attention were the southernmost escort carrier unit, Taffy 1. Four Zeros from Davao, most likely from the *Wakazakura* unit, attacked at 0740hrs. They were later joined by two other Zeros from the *Yamato* unit in an attack described above in the Introduction.

At 1050hrs, it was the turn of the *Shikishima* unit, five kamikaze A6M2 Zeros accompanied by and three A6Ms serving as escorts. The escort was led by Nishizawa Hiroyoshi, an ace with an eventual 86 kills to his credit. The aircraft departed Mabalacat, being seen off by Admiral Ōnishi, and encountered Taffy 3 as Kurita was returning to the San Bernardino Strait. Thinking they had found a unit of the Fast Carrier Task Force, they attacked the carriers.

Two planes launched dives on USS *White Plains*, approaching it from astern. Antiaircraft fire damaged one of the Zeros. Its pilot may have believed he could not reach *White Plains*, and altered course heading for the *St Lo*. The second kamikaze was destroyed by antiaircraft fire mere yards from the carrier. It disintegrated, showering *White Plains* with debris and causing minor damage.

Meanwhile, the first Zero successfully crashed into *St Lo*, smashing through the flight deck aft. It burst into flames, which detonated torpedoes and bombs in the hangar, brought up to arm aircraft attacking Kurita's ships. A series of explosions rocked the *St Lo*. Nine minutes later, at 1100hrs, *St Lo*'s captain ordered the ship to be abandoned. Twenty-three minutes on, it capsized and sank.

Three other Zeros then attacked *Kalinin Bay*, the trailing carrier in Taffy 3, whose antiaircraft gunners shot down two of them. One of the Zeros smashed into the port side of the flight deck, while the third clipped *Kalinin Bay*'s aft funnel. The flight deck hit caused fires to break out, but these were quenched within minutes. The *Shikishima* unit's escort flight returned to base reporting three fleet carriers hit, with two sunk.

To compound Taffy 3's misery, 15 D4Ys came across the carrier unit at 1108hrs. This was not a kamikaze unit; rather they were conventional bombers. The bombers were intercepted by Wildcats launched from USS *Kitkun Bay*, two D4Ys being shot down by CAP. At least one of the remaining bombers, perhaps inspired by the example of the *Shikishima* aircraft, decided to emulate them, diving on *Kitkun Bay*. Antiaircraft fire severed the wings from the D4Y before it reached the carrier; its bomb splashed into the sea 25 yards ahead of *Kitkun Bay*'s starboard bow, with pieces of the stricken aircraft scattered over the carrier's forecastle.

By the time October 25 ended, six escort carriers had been hit by kamikazes. Only one of these had sunk, the others being back in action, conducting flight operations, although the *Suwannee*, *Santee*, and *Kalinin Bay* needed dockyard attention. Japanese escort pilots returning from the strikes reported six fleet aircraft carriers hit, with three certainly sunk and one possibly sunk.

The overstated losses to the Allied carriers was an understandable error on the part of the Japanese. It was difficult for even experienced observers (as these escort pilots were) to differentiate between an escort carrier in a formation of escort carriers from a fleet carrier in

Attacks on two escort carrier units on October 25, 1944, led the US Navy to realize Japanese aircraft were deliberately crashing on Allied ships. Although several escort carriers were hit that day, the kamikaze shown diving on the *Kitkun Bay* missed hitting it. (AC)

In November 1944, kamikazes turned their attention to the freighters supplying the US forces which landed on Leyte. On November 12, no fewer than nine large cargo ships were struck by kamikazes while offshore. (USNHHC)

a formation of fleet carriers. From 18,000ft, the altitude the attacks started, it was hard to tell apart an 800ft fleet carrier and a 500–600ft escort carrier, especially as both had similar length-to-breadth ratios.

The hits had caused massive fires on four of the escort carriers. The escort aircraft departed soon after the strike planes had been expended, when the fires were not yet under control. Underestimating US Navy damage control capabilities, they understandably believed all four of the blazing carriers were finished.

The reported results elated Ōnishi. Even discounting the claims of three carriers sunk, measuring the fires observed against Imperial Navy damage control standards, Ōnishi would have believed all four were out of the battle. This meant the US Fast Carrier Task Force had lost one-quarter of its carriers in a single day. For him, it vindicated the sacrifices made by the kamikazes.

As dawn broke on October 26, the Allied fleet wondered what the suicidal attacks of the previous day meant. They had occurred within the larger context of the battle of Leyte Gulf, in which Japan threw two battleship forces and a carrier force against the invasion beachhead. Was it possible this was a one-off event supporting that effort, or were the Japanese introducing man-piloted bombs to the war?

The answer came shortly after noon, when the First Kamikaze Special Attack Group struck again. Taffy 1 had just endured a conventional attack by D4Ys, which was largely neutralized by the carrier unit's CAP. That distraction allowed five kamikaze Zeros escorted by three other Zeros, all from the *Yamato* unit, to slip through. One Zeke hit USS *Suwannee*, crashing into a just-recovered antisubmarine patrol Avenger sitting on the elevator. Both planes exploded, killing all four airmen. The blast ignited nine armed aircraft on the flight deck, which in turn exploded. The fire was only brought under control after a tough multi-hour flight. The *Suwannee* lost 85 dead, 58 missing, and 102 wounded; 20 percent casualties. But it had been lucky: the depth charge aboard the first Avenger hit only burned instead of exploding.

Over the next three days, the remaining aircraft of the First Kamikaze were expended. Taffy 3 and the damaged ships of Taffy 1 of the Escort Carrier Force withdrew to rearm and refit at Ulithi. The Fast Carrier Task Force moved to cover the Leyte beaches until they returned. On October 27, two Zeros attacked the Fast Carrier Task Force, but were shot down. Three more Zeros from the First Kamikaze attacked the Fast Carrier Task Force on October 29, and the final six came down the following day, after which the First Kamikaze Group was disbanded.

The success of the First Kamikaze Group led almost immediately to the creation of a second *tokko* formation, the Second Kamikaze Special Attack Group. This formation was drawn from Navy bomber formations in the Philippines, mainly the 701st Naval Air Group, comprising Aichi D3As and Yokosuka D4Ys. It launched its first attacks on October 27, expending all but one aircraft by November 1.

The Second Kamikaze first strikes concentrated on the cargo ships supporting the Leyte invasion. On October 27, five D4Ys and six D3As struck US shipping, attacking in groups of two or three. The attacks were more frightening than effective, with 11 kamikazes managing only one hit. One crashed into a cargo hold of the Liberty ship *Benjamin Ide Wheeler*. It blew a hole in the bottom of the ship, which sank in 36ft of water. This left its guns above water, which continued shooting. The ship was later refloated and used as a stationary depot ship. The remaining kamikazes were shot down, as was a lone D3A which attacked the transports the following day.

The US fast carriers launched a series of strikes on October 29 designed to close down enemy-held Luzon airfields. The strikes achieved one of their objectives, to denude the Japanese in the Philippines of aircraft. Nearly 90 planes were destroyed: 13 on the ground and 73 in the air. The carrier attacks also brought them close enough for the kamikazes to strike.

The rest of the Second Kamikaze, joined by remnants of the First Kamikaze, was spent attacking the Fast Carrier Task Force. They threw 15 kamikazes at the fleet on October 29; three Zeros from the First Kamikaze, and two D4Ys and ten D3As from the Second, again attacking in twos and threes. Yet all these aircraft mustered only one hit between them, the rest being shot down by CAP or antiaircraft fire. USS *Intrepid*, a fleet carrier, was hit by a kamikaze which inflicted just light damage while killing ten and wounding six of *Intrepid*'s crew.

On November 1, the *Abner Read* was struck and sunk by a kamikaze while the Fletcher-class destroyer was guarding cargo ships in Leyte Gulf. Three other US destroyers were hit and damaged on the same day. (USNHHC)

The IJA joined the kamikaze effort in the second week of November 1944. Here, an Army Ki-48 crashes into the water short of its intended target, from which the photograph was taken. (AC)

The next day, five of the six remaining A6Ms from the First Kamikaze Group eluded CAP and attacked TG38.4. Three were shot down by flak during their dive, but one struck the Essex-class *Franklin*, destroying 33 aircraft on the carrier, knocking the aft elevator out of commission, and opening a 40ft hole in its deck. Casualties from the strike numbered 56 dead and 14 seriously wounded. The final Zero crashed into the light carrier *Belleau Wood*, whose flight deck was cratered, with 14 aircraft destroyed, 92 crew killed, and 14 wounded. Fires badly damaged the *Belleau Wood* before they were brought under control. The *Franklin* and *Belleau Wood* left for repairs in Ulithi the next day.

On November 1, the Second Kamikaze turned its attention back to Leyte Gulf and the Tacloban beaches. It was accompanied by the newly formed Third and Fourth Kamikaze Special Attack Groups. The Third Kamikaze was largely created from surviving aircraft of the First Air Fleet's fighter squadrons, the units from which the First Kamikaze had been formed, plus volunteers from First Air Fleet strike squadrons. It comprised A6Ms and D4Ys. The group would be reinforced in November by volunteers from the Second Air Fleet. The Fourth Kamikaze, meanwhile, was drawn from reinforcements sent to the Philippines.

US airpower was at its nadir as November opened. The only airfield on the beachhead, Tacloban Field, was stuffed to its limited capacity. Most of the carrier groups, both fast and escort, had withdrawn to Ulithi. Those carriers not needing repairs desperately needed resupply and maintenance. CAP was consequently light.

Over the next two days, the kamikazes reaped a savage harvest. There were no aircraft carriers available, so they concentrated on the invasion support ships and their escorts. Conventional aircraft also joined in the battle. At 0950hrs on November 1, a D4Y dived from the clouds onto the destroyer USS *Claxton*. The plane exploded in the water beside the *Claxton*, knocking a hole in its side, flooding its living quarters, killing five crew and wounding 23.

Two minutes later, a P1Y1, one of several launching conventional attacks, became an impromptu kamikaze after being severely damaged. It dived into the destroyer *Ammen*. It hit *Ammen's* superstructure at the bridge, but bounced off, landing in the ocean. Considerable damage was done, with three killed and 21 wounded.

Conventional bombers damaged two other US destroyers between 0940hrs and 1200hrs, but no further kamikazes struck until 1330hrs. Then, two D3As from the Fourth Kamikaze plunged out of the sky at the USS *Abner Read*. The lead plane struck the destroyer, starting a fire which caused its magazines to explode. The ship rolled over and sank at 1415hrs, 17 minutes after the crew were ordered to abandon ship. The destroyers *Leary* and the previously damaged *Claxton* rescued all but 22 of the *Abner Read*'s crew.

At 1812hrs, the final kamikaze of the day hit the Sims-class destroyer *Anderson*. The attacks were renewed on November 3, when two cargo ships off Tacloban – SS *Cape Constance* and the Liberty ship *Matthew P. Deady* – were damaged by kamikazes.

The Japanese Second Air Fleet reached the Philippines in late October. Its commander initially resisted developing *tokko* units, preferring conventional air attack, which offered an opportunity to use crews and aircraft on multiple missions, although they did provide escorts to First Air Fleet kamikazes. A few of its pilots conducted spontaneous kamikaze attacks, regardless. By the end of the first week of November, the Second Air Fleet also began organizing *tokko* units.

The first Second Air Fleet *tokko* joined First Air Fleet units as part of the Third Kamikaze attacks on the Fast Carrier Task Force on November 5. TF38 was striking airfields on Luzon and shipping around Luzon's waters when four A6Ms evaded the carriers' CAP and struck TG38.3. Three Zeros were shot down, but one hit USS *Lexington* on its island aft, killing 50 crew, injuring 132 – many seriously – and starting fires that took 20 minutes to douse. The *Lexington* kept up with the Task Force, but required repairs when it arrived at Ulithi on November 9.

Throughout mid-November, kamikazes were an all-Navy show. At this stage, pilots were enthusiastically volunteering as kamikazes, even though sometimes the volunteers were pilots Japan could ill-afford to lose. Nishizawa Hiroyoshi, who escorted the first kamikaze mission,

When TF38 attacked Luzon on November 25, 1944, kamikazes struck back against them. A kamikaze is photographed disintegrating in a fiery explosion after hitting the flight deck of USS *Intrepid*. (AC)

repeatedly volunteered. Viewed as too valuable to lose, he was ordered out of the Philippines to preserve him.

The Imperial Japanese Army's aircraft had not yet participated, even though it established the *Banda* and *Fugaku* units in the summer. These consisted of 12 specially converted Ki-48 and Ki-67 twin-engine bombers, respectively. Navy success prompted the Army to commit these units to combat, and to organize an additional 18 *tokko* units in November with a further 216 aircraft.

The Imperial Japanese Navy renewed its kamikaze attacks on supply ships supporting the Leyte landing on November 11. The *Banda* and *Fugaku* units joined in a few days later. Four D3As and a D4Y attacked on November 11, without scoring hits. The Third Kamikaze threw 19 Zeros and the *Banda* unit of four Ki-48s at the ships the next day, hitting and damaging seven ships: six Liberty ships and the USS *Achilles*, an LST converted to a repair ship. Two of the Liberty ships were carrying troops, 350 of whom died in the kamikaze strikes.

The Fast Carrier Task Force appeared off Luzon the following day, launching two days of air strikes on Japanese airfields and shipping which drew the kamikazes away from the cargo ships. The Japanese threw most of the *Fugaku* Ki-67s and four Navy kamikazes against the carriers without scoring a hit. Maneuvering 30-knot carriers proved harder to hit than anchored transports.

The kamikazes returned their attention to the invasion support shipping on November 15. Between then and November 23, they struck again at Leyte Gulf. Six more cargo ships were hit and damaged, including two transports. The damage was the product of only 20 kamikaze aircraft, split evenly between the Navy and Army. Most attacks were made at night, and were conducted individually. As November waned, it was becoming apparent the IJA had lost its battle for Leyte, and was withdrawing. This meant that attacking the support ships was becoming less important, so kamikazes were directed towards other targets.

These other targets included the Big Blue Fleet in the last week of November. TF38, which was working over Luzon every week or so, launched another set of strikes on November 25. This time, only two carrier task groups participated, the other two being tied up with other operations or refitting. This meant fewer aircraft were available for CAP and for hitting Japanese airfields. Their primary targets were whatever Japanese warships and shipping still remained in the vicinity of Luzon. Airfield attacks and fighter sweeps concentrated on northern Luzon, with only cursory coverage of Luzon's southeastern tail.

As before, the kamikazes went after the carriers once made aware of their presence by US carrier airstrikes around Luzon. The strikes all originated from the same patch of ocean east of Luzon, so the Japanese knew

A flaming D4Y bomber is captured just before crashing into the aircraft carrier *Essex* on November 25, 1944. (AC)

where to send their aircraft. What kamikazes they had were clustered in southern Luzon for access to Leyte Gulf.

Both carrier task groups were targeted. TG38.2, which had the Essex-class *Hancock* and *Intrepid* and light carrier *Cabot*, came under attack at 1229hrs. Six Zeros constituted the first wave, two of which were shot down by CAP. The others slipped through, and at 1234hrs, one dived on the *Hancock*. Antiaircraft fire disintegrated the fighter 300ft above the carrier, but debris rained on the flight deck, starting a small fire and knocking out a 20mm gun.

At 1248hrs, a second strike of ten Zeros swept in. This time one kamikaze hit the *Intrepid* and another struck the *Cabot*, while a third had a near miss against the latter. USS *Intrepid* was hit on the gallery deck, just below the flight deck, starting serious fires. The *Cabot*, meanwhile, ended up with two big holes in its flight deck, a gash in the hull, 36 men killed, and 16 seriously wounded.

TG38.2 endured another strike just before 1300hrs, when a kamikaze struck *Intrepid* from the stern. The plane came in at a shallow angle, with the engine and cockpit skidding down the length of the flight deck. Its bomb punched through the flight deck, exploding on the hangar deck. Fires quickly started, filling the flight deck with dense smoke. While soon brought under control, damage to the flight deck made it impossible for *Intrepid* to continue flight operations.

TG38.3's turn came at 1255hrs. While USS *Essex* was launching aircraft, two kamikazes dived on it. One was shot down, but the other hit on the forward flight deck, on the port side, killing 15 crew but not causing any serious damage. With the kamikaze attacks terminated,

# Bullseye

The kamikaze campaign was just a month old on November 25, 1944. The Japanese main target was the US Navy's Fast Carrier Task Force, a target which largely eluded the Japanese through most of the opening days of the campaign. There had been a few attacks, but most of the carriers hit by kamikazes between October 26 and November 25 had been escort carriers. Attacks against fast carriers had yielded only one hit, that on the Essex-class *Yorktown* on November 5. But on November 25, Japan spun fortune's wheel and scored big.

TF38 was making a third visit to a patch of ocean off Luzon's eastern coast to attack naval targets around Luzon. The Japanese had noticed the fast carriers were returning to that area every seven days to launch airstrikes. They maintained air searches over the area during the days the US carriers were expected to show up, and found them.

This time it was the US Navy that got caught napping. Since only two of TF38's three carrier groups were present, US resources were stretched, with fewer fighters available for CAP and fighter sweeps concentrated on the airfields around Luzon.

The Japanese launched a series of kamikaze raids in the late morning of November 25. Moreover, the kamikazes came from southern Luzon airfields rather than those near Manila, where the US fighters were hunting. Between 1230hrs and 1330hrs, both US carrier groups were attacked by three waves of kamikazes. By the time the attacks ended, four carriers had been struck: the Essex-class fleet carriers *Essex*, *Intrepid*, and *Hancock*, and the light carrier *Cabot*.

The *Cabot* was more vulnerable than its bigger fleet counterparts. Built on light cruiser hulls, light carriers had less margin and less defensive capabilities than fleet carriers. They displaced half the tonnage of the fleet carriers and carried a much weaker antiaircraft battery: they had no 5in. guns, and one-third of the 40mm armament carried by the Essex-class ships. It was therefore hard for a light carrier to stop an inbound kamikaze.

So it proved on November 25, when a kamikaze bore in on the carrier just before 1300hrs. The *Cabot* opened up with all of its 40mm Bofors in an attempt to stop it, but could not put enough steel in the air between it and the oncoming kamikaze. Although the aircraft took several hits, none were able to stop the aircraft. Momentum moved it relentlessly forward, and it smashed into the *Cabot* on the forward flight deck on the port side. It knocked a 6ft hole in the flight deck, and took out the port catwalk and part of the forward gun gallery.

Minutes later, a second kamikaze dived at the *Cabot*. This time, the carrier's antiaircraft fire forced a miss and the kamikaze splashed into the water nearby.

This plate shows the first kamikaze seconds before it strikes. The gun crews kept up their fire hoping for a lucky, last-minute hit. Meanwhile, flight deck crew members scattered, attempting to get clear of the onrushing aircraft.

*Intrepid*'s aircraft aloft landed on the *Essex*, *Ticonderoga*, and *Hancock*. A strike on shipping around the Visayas planned for the next day was canceled, with TF38 retiring to Ulithi.

The kamikazes closed out the month with strikes on the Seventh Fleet's fire support warships on November 27 and 29, when the subchaser SC-744, mistaken for a larger vessel, was hit and sunk. The battleships *Colorado* and *Maryland*, light cruisers *Denver*, *Montpelier*, and *St Louis*, and three destroyers were all hit, with damage ranging from light to serious, although the cruisers and battleships were able to continue their support operations.

## Countering the kamikazes: December 1, 1944–January 13, 1945

Japan was reinforcing its kamikaze units in late November and early December. News of the campaign was raising homeland morale, with kamikaze stories filling newspapers and radio broadcasts. Pictured as a complete success, its sacrificial spirit was used to inspire Japanese factory workers and farmers to redouble their efforts and thus become figurative production kamikazes by showing the same zeal as the kamikaze pilots.

Kamikaze tactics were seemingly effective. Pilots assumed all of the blazing carriers they observed following strikes had sunk, and the commanders in turn accepted these estimates – in part because rejecting them would be seen as devaluing the sacrifices made by kamikazes. If the success claims were true, kamikazes would have reduced the enemy's fast carriers (it was assumed kamikazes *always* attacked fast carriers) by nearly a dozen.

However, the assessment was overoptimistic, but the alternative was conceding that the kamikazes' sacrifices had been vain, and Japan was still unwilling to accept that reality. To many, the Fast Carrier Task Force's long battlefield absence following the November 25 kamikaze attacks seemed to indicate that just maybe damage to the US carriers was not overstated.

In reality, rather than licking its wounds, the Big Blue Fleet was taking a break, planning what it would do next to fight the kamikazes. On October 30, Vice Admiral John S. McCain

One change instituted in December 1944 was doubling the number of fighters aboard US fleet carriers. This increased air defense against kamikazes without sacrificing offensive capability. The F6F and F4U could double as bombers, carrying almost as big a load as Avengers and Helldivers. (AC)

replaced Admiral Marc Mitscher as commander of TF 38, when Mitscher was reassigned to command TF58. The transfer occurred during the middle of operations supporting the Leyte invasion. Requirements of the Leyte operation kept the Fast Carrier Task Force too busy to permit much more than minor changes to organizational structure and tactics.

The November 25 raid ended the US Third Fleet's support of the Leyte operation. As November ended, progress on the Leyte airfields permitted the USAAF to operate enough aircraft to assume responsibility for protecting the skies over the island. Thereafter, air and naval support for Leyte became the responsibility of the Seventh Fleet and the USAAF, allowing the Third Fleet to prepare future operations against Mindoro and Luzon.

McCain and his staff had been absorbing the lessons of the kamikaze campaign throughout November, using the break at Ulithi to make changes. The carriers were rearranged into three task groups of four or five aircraft carriers, typically two or three fleet carriers and two light carriers. Casualties from the opening of the kamikaze campaign had temporarily reduced the Fast Carrier Task Force to seven fleet and six light carriers at the start of December: The Essex-class fleet carriers *Yorktown*, *Wasp*, *Lexington*, *Hancock*, *Hornet*, *Essex*, and *Ticonderoga* and light carriers *Cowpens*, *Monterey*, *Independence*, *Cabot*, *Langley*, and *San Jacinto*.

The *Enterprise* was undergoing conversion to a night-operations carrier (joining the light carrier *Independence* in that role), while the Essex-class *Franklin* and *Intrepid* and Independence-class *Belleau Wood* were undergoing major repairs. More fleet carriers, including pre-war *Saratoga* and new-construction Essex-class carriers, would join the Fast Carrier Task Force before the war ended in August, while other carriers would depart for repairs as they became damaged. Throughout this time, the carrier force bounced between 12 and 20 fast carriers.

Another change made during this break was increasing the number of fighters carried. This increased the ability to provide CAP and fighter sweeps, both of which were already recognized as critical in defeating kamikazes. The excess Helldivers were transferred to shore-based squadrons, while the Avengers were split between shore-based units or fed into the ever-growing pool of escort carriers.

To counter the successful Japanese tactic of sneaking kamikazes into groups of the returning carrier aircraft, Tom Cat destroyers were instituted with delousing air patrols over them. Radar tracking techniques were also refined, to better detect individual kamikazes seeking to reach the Big Blue Fleet. Additionally, night carrier operations were expanded to guard against night kamikazes, including converting a fleet carrier (*Enterprise*) to exclusive night operations.

The Third Fleet's break was supposed to end on December 1, after which the Big Blue Fleet was to have sailed to support the Mindoro invasion originally scheduled for December 5. However, the invasion was postposed to December 15, just as the Third Fleet was leaving Ulithi, so the ships returned to Ulithi for ten days of additional upkeep. The extra time allowed McCain's staff to perfect another proposed counter to the kamikazes, the "Big Blue Blanket," which TF38 hoped to try out for the forthcoming Mindoro invasion.

With the Third Fleet absent, Japan's *tokko* forces returned to Leyte Gulf, having taken a one-week break after the November 29 attacks on the Seventh Fleet. This time, cargo ships and transports were the main target. On December 5, a dozen kamikazes went after a convoy approaching Leyte. Five US ships were hit, with two Liberty ships damaged, one badly, as was the intermediate landing ship LSM-23.

LSM-20 was less fortunate: struck by a kamikaze amidships, it sank in 20 minutes after the aircraft's bomb exploded in the engine room. USS *Mugford*, a Bagley-class destroyer, was also hit. Seeing the convoy under attack, the *Mugford* went to assist the ships, only to be hit by a Ki-43. With eight crew killed and 14 wounded, it was so badly damaged it remained out of combat until March 1945.

LSM-20, headed for the Ormac beachhead on December 5, 1944, was in the Surigao Strait when it was struck by a kamikaze and sunk. (USNHHC)

On December 6, it was the Mahan-class USS *Drayton*'s turn, a twin-engine bomber narrowly missing the destroyer. The next day, an A6M smashed into its forward turret. The two attacks killed eight aboard and wounded 19.

The *Drayton* was only one among several ships hit on Pearl Harbor's third anniversary. The Allies, attempting to clean up Leyte, landed at Ormoc Bay on Leyte's west coast. Shortly after troops were landed, a swarm of kamikazes attacked the invasion force. Over three dozen aircraft attacked, including a half-dozen P1Y1s and a dozen each A6Ms, Ki-43s, and Ki-45s. Eight ships were hit, with three vessels sunk.

Hardest hit were the transports, fortunately unloaded of troops when the attacks began. LSM-318 was sunk, as were two other LSMs and an LCT (Landing Craft Tank). Two high-speed transports, USS *Liddle* and USS *Ward*, were also hit. The *Liddle*, converted from a destroyer escort, was attacked by five kamikazes. Hit on the bridge by one, the ship lost 38 of its crew killed or severely wounded. The converted flush-deck destroyer *Ward* was hit amidships by a twin-engine bomber, and sank three years to the day after it fired the first shot of the Pacific War at Pearl Harbor.

The destroyer *Mahan*, another venerable veteran, was also sunk in these attacks. Nine bombers and four fighters attacked it, and while the *Mahan* shot down four, it was hit by three. The rest were downed or driven off by USAAF fighters. Ablaze with uncontrollable fires, *Mahan*'s captain ordered it to be abandoned; it was subsequently sunk by other US destroyers.

This attack was notable for its size, one of the biggest in the Philippines phase of the campaign and one of the first times kamikazes used such mass-attack tactics. It was also the first major use of low-level kamikaze tactics, with most of the kamikazes approaching as if making torpedo attacks, before climbing for a terminal dive on the target.

On December 10, kamikazes targeted the east side of Leyte. Two Liberty ships unloading off Dulag were hit: one, SS *William S. Ladd*, carrying ammunition and aviation gasoline, exploded and sank. A kamikaze which missed the *Ladd* struck and sank *LCT-1075*. Four kamikazes also jumped two PT boats patrolling Leyte Gulf, managing to hit and sink *PT-323*. USS *Hughes*, also patrolling in Leyte Gulf, was attacked by Ki-45s, being struck in the engine room and badly damaged.

The next day, another Mahan-class destroyer, USS *Reid*, was sunk when a convoy of amphibious ships resupplying the Ormoc beachhead was attacked by 12 kamikazes in the Surigao Straits. The *Reid*, escorting the ships, was the nearest to the kamikazes and the largest ship in the convoy. Seven kamikazes attacked it, and in less than a minute, the *Reid* shot down three attackers before being struck by four other aircraft. The last aircraft's bomb struck *Reid's* aft magazine, which exploded; the ship sank, taking with it 103 members of its crew. Benson-class destroyer *Caldwell* attracted the attention of the remaining kamikazes, one of which crashed into its bridge, killing 33 crew and wounding 40 more. Only effective damage control saved the *Caldwell* from sinking.

Mindoro, an island near Luzon due south of Manila, had been chosen as the site of the next major Allied amphibious operation in the Philippines. This assault bypassed garrisons on Japanese-held islands closer to Allied-occupied Leyte. Only lightly held, Mindoro offered a good spot for airfields conveniently close to provide air support for the planned invasion of Luzon.

On December 13, Seventh Fleet forces entered the Sulu Sea to support the scheduled landing at Mindoro two days later. The Mindoro Attack Group, with some 80 amphibious warfare ships, was escorted by the light cruiser *Nashville*, 12 destroyers, and the Heavy Covering and Carrier Group, which included six escort carriers. Over the next three days, it served as the focus of attention for Japanese kamikazes attempting to prevent the landings.

On December 13, four Zeros found the Mindoro Attack Group. One of the aircraft, carrying two bombs, struck the *Nashville* on its port side. Both bombs penetrated, and the strike started fires which began setting off antiaircraft ammunition. By the time the fires were brought under control, 133 crew were dead and 190 wounded. Meanwhile, seven kamikazes, including twin-engine Ki-48s, attacked the covering group. CAP accounted for four of them. Of the remaining three, two were shot

Even when kamikazes were absent, they exerted a psychological toll on the sailors of the Allied fleets. Here, the gun crews from a US Navy light cruiser guarding the Mindoro invasion anxiously scan the sky for kamikazes. (AC)

**OPPOSITE** KAMIKAZE ATTACKS IN THE PHILIPPINES

down and one crashed into the Fletcher-class *Haraden*, leaving it dead in the water. Both the badly damaged US warships required extensive periods of repair.

This was the apogee of kamikaze attacks in the Philippines. By December 15, more than half of Japan's air strength in the Philippines was committed to *tokko* combat. At the time, it appeared to be a winning strategy. Although the Japanese had been unsuccessful in keeping the Allies from taking Leyte, they planned to stop the Mindoro invasion through a massive air attack on the Allied fleet, involving nearly 200 aircraft, on December 14.

However, having sailed from Ulithi on December 11 to cover the Mindoro landings, the reappearance of the US Third Fleet checkmated the Japanese plan. It was the first field-test of the Big Blue Blanket, which dropped over Luzon on December 14. At 0715hrs, 29 IJA aircraft and 40 IJN aircraft – of which 49 were kamikazes – rose from airfields around Manila, running into the initial fighter sweeps being conducted by TF38. Two-thirds of the Japanese aircraft which headed for the invasion fleet were shot down. The survivors failed to find the Mindoro Attack Group: assuming the landings were intended for Negros or Panay, they searched the wrong patch of ocean.

These aircraft were forced to land at Cebu and Davao on Mindanao. They could not return to Luzon, where TF38 aircraft owned the skies. For three days, TF38 opened each day with a fighter sweep, aimed at clearing the skies of any airborne Japanese aircraft. Thereafter, carrier aircraft maintained 24-hour air patrols over every suspected Japanese airfield on Luzon.

During daylight hours, carrier fighters hovered over their assigned field ready to pounce on any aircraft attempting to take off. Carrier night fighter units continued coverage during the hours of darkness. In the intervals when a new fighter patrol relieved an existing one, the airfield was bombed by Avengers and Helldivers carrying fragmentation or high-explosive bombs intended to destroy aircraft and crater runways.

Twenty kamikazes made it to the Mindoro invasion beaches on December 15, 1944. They hit and sank two LSTs, including *LST-472*, shown blazing as crews from surrounding ships attempt to bring the fires under control. (AC)

Ships damaged
Ships sunk
Major Japanese airfields

**Events**
1. Leyte invasion: October 20, 1944
2. Ormoc Bay landings: December 7, 1944
3. Mindoro landings: December 13, 1944
4. Lingayen Gulf landings: January 6, 1945

Laoag
Aparri
Vigan

*Lingayen Gulf*

Luzon

4
Lingayen

Clark

*Philippine Sea*

Manila
**Nichols**

*South China Sea*

Naga
Legazpi

*San Bernadino Strait*

Mindoro

Samar

3

*Sibuyan Sea*

Masbate

Tacloban
1

2

Panay

Iloilo

Cebu
Cebu **Lahug**

Leyte

*Surigao Strait*

Palawan

Negros

Puerto Princesa

*Sulu Sea*

Mindanao

N

0            100 miles

0            100km

Cotabato

**Matina**

**San Roque**
Zamboanga

Davao

There were constant adjustments to the coverage during those three days. Some fields were found to be empty and inoperable, while other previously reported fields proved nonexistent. Aircraft originally intended to cover these empty or abandoned airfields were shifted to more fruitful targets. The carriers also interdicted the air routes from Formosa to Luzon, hindering Japanese attempts to reinforce their aerial forces in the Philippines.

Nor was TF38 alone in its suppression efforts. On December 14, a Marine Corsair squadron at Leyte attacked Masbate, while another shut down southern Luzon's Naga airfield. The six escort carriers with the invasion covering force launched their own fighter sweeps over Panay's San José and Negros's Don Hermanos airfields. Those, too, were closed down.

TF38 flew 1,671 mostly fighter sorties during its raids from December 14–16. There were only 244 bomber sorties flown and 336 tons of bombs dropped. The raids destroyed around 175 Japanese aircraft, three-quarters of which were lost on the ground. The most important result was at the Mindoro beachhead, where save for the attacks on December 14, no ship of the Mindoro Attack Group was attacked by kamikazes from Luzon until after the troops carried were unloaded.

This did not mean they completely escaped kamikaze attacks. Airfields in Cebu, Mindanao, and Palawan fell outside the smothering coverage of the Big Blue Blanket. South of Mindoro, the skies were largely the responsibility of the Seventh Fleet's escort carriers, which were fewer than the fast carriers, carried fewer aircraft per carrier, and split responsibility between air cover and ground support. That made the skies to the south more porous, allowing a small number of kamikazes to leak through.

The worst day was December 15, when six ships were hit by kamikazes. A Japanese patrol aircraft finally spotted the invasion force off Mindoro that morning at 0530hrs. Between 30 and 40 Japanese aircraft then took off to attack, with roughly half of them kamikazes, most from Davao.

The attacks opened at 0812hrs, when between eight and ten kamikazes targeted the escort carrier group. First of all, a P1Y1 made a run at USS *Ralph Talbot*. Shot down, it disintegrated 300 yards from the destroyer, which was sprayed by flaming debris. Another screening destroyer, the *Howorth*, was also lightly damaged, and two LSTs and three Liberty ships were sunk.

CAP nailed a second kamikaze, and then two P1Y1s made low-level attacks on the escort carrier *Marcus Island*. Both near-missed after being shot down, one ahead of and one behind

While the "Big Blue Blanket" shut down kamikazes from Luzon during the invasion of Mindoro, its coverage did not extend to the Philippines' other islands, especially Mindanao. One of the kamizazes that leaked through is shown attacking the escort carrier *Marcus Island*. This P1Y1 barely missed astern. (AC)

the carrier, which suffered minor damage. Between 0900hrs and 1000hrs, six more kamikazes attacked the escort group, only to be shot down or driven off by CAP and antiaircraft fire.

More serious was an attack by 20 more kamikazes at around 1000hrs. They spotted the amphibious force off the southern two landing beaches and charged in. Half were intercepted and shot down by CAP. LST-472 and LST-738 were sunk by the rest, but not before the former shot down four of the five kamikazes attacking it. Neither ship had unloaded, but they were the only pre-invasion kamikaze casualties.

The Japanese did not ease up on Mindoro in the three weeks that followed. The IJA and IJN sent over 50 kamikazes in total to hit the ships carrying supplies and reinforcements to Mindoro's beachheads, striking 15 ships in and around Mindoro, six of them warships. One PT boat was sunk, while another PT and four destroyers were damaged; the rest were support ships. Four LSTs (including one converted to a PT-boat tender) and four Liberty ships were sunk, while three other Liberty ships were damaged.

The Japanese saved the worst for last, hitting SS *Lewis L. Dyche*, which was loaded with ammunition, on January 4, 1945. The explosion obliterated the Liberty ship, killing all aboard. Falling debris damaged a nearby fleet oiler and minelayer.

Despite these losses, the warships hit were only minor combatants, while the logistics ships and their cargos were replaceable. Japan sacrificed nearly 80 aircraft (including those supporting the kamikazes) and their crews in exchange for this paltry result. The only reason the Japanese got so many kamikazes through was that they attacked during the pauses when the Big Blue Blanket was lifted, with TF38 on other assignments. The kamikaze attacks did not stop or even seriously slow the occupation of Mindoro or the construction of Allied airfields there. Events at Mindoro demonstrated that kamikazes could at best only delay the Allied advance; they could not halt or reverse it.

Japanese attention was drawn away from Mindoro in early 1945 by a more urgent problem: the Allies were invading Luzon, the key to the Philippines. Luzon is the archipelago's largest island, containing its largest city and capital, Manila. The Japanese knew Leyte and Mindoro were only precursors to the Luzon landings.

The Allied landings occurred on the opposite side of Luzon from Mindoro, at Lingayen Gulf. It was the obvious invasion site on Luzon; Japan had used the location in its December 1941 invasion of Luzon. By 1945, being the obvious location mattered less than the advantages of the site, as it offered quick access to Clark Field, the heart of Japan's aircraft defense on Luzon. Just beyond the airfield was the "Pearl of the Orient," Manila.

The landings occurred on January 6, but both sides had set their forces in motion the previous week. On January 3, three kamikazes hit a Seventh Fleet supply task group heading towards Lingayen Gulf as it traveled through the Sulu Sea. A Zero hit the fleet oiler *Cowanesque*, but damage control doused the resulting fire and the bomb carried failed to explode. *Cowanesque* was able to complete its mission.

Less lucky was the escort carrier *Ommaney Bay*, with TG77.4, the escort carriers assigned to support the invasion. Several IJN Ki-45s from Mindanao evaded USAAF patrols and found the Seventh Fleet south and west of Mindoro, with Panay and the Cuyo islands hiding the approaching aircraft from the task force's radar. One dived on USS *Ommaney Bay*, undetected until too late. One bomb penetrated to the second deck of the carrier before exploding in the engine room and depressurizing the fire mains. Damage control was consequently unable to contain the fires, and *Ommaney Bay* was abandoned and sunk. By now alerted to the threat, antiaircraft gunners stopped subsequent attackers that day.

As the Seventh Fleet steamed up Luzon's west coast on January 5, the Japanese realized it was headed for Lingayen Gulf to mount an invasion. The Japanese threw everything they had at the Allies, but they had pitifully few airplanes. Three waves of aircraft attacked the main body: the first at 0800hrs, then at 1130hrs, and 1650hrs. Only the third wave – 20 Zeros, 16 of them kamikazes – broke through. The first two, consisting of 30 IJA aircraft

## OPPOSITE TF38 THROWS THE "BIG BLUE BLANKET" OVER THE KAMIKAZES

The "Big Blue Blanket," developed by "Jimmy" Thatch, doused kamikaze attacks by smothering all airfields from which they might launch with round-the-clock coverage by US Navy carrier aircraft. First tried during the Mindoro invasion, it worked well, despite the difficulty of maintaining it over an island as large and with as many airfields as Luzon. During the duration of the Big Blue Blanket – December 14–16 – no kamikazes attacked the Mindoro convoys from Luzon.

The invasion fleet in Lingayen Gulf. The skies are filled with antiaircraft bursts intended to check the efforts of kamikazes attempting to defeat the invasion. (AC)

including seven kamikazes, were intercepted before reaching the task force and turned away with heavy casualties.

Nine Allied ships – all warships – were hit and damaged in the attacks by the third wave. Heading the list were the heavy cruisers *Louisville* and *Australia*. Neither was seriously damaged, but they lost 26 crewmen killed and 90 wounded between them, most of the dead on the *Australia*. The escort carriers *Savo Island* and *Manila Bay* were also hit. Although the *Savo Island* escaped with light damage, *Manila Bay*, hit by two kamikazes, took a day to resume limited flight operations; not until January 9 did it resume full operations. The Australian destroyer *Arunta* and US destroyer *Helm* and destroyer escort *Stafford* were also damaged in the strikes. Damage to the destroyers was slight, while the *Stafford* suffered a flooded engine room but was towed to safety.

A little later, at 1715hrs, the minesweeping group TG77.6, independently leading the main body, was attacked by a small group of kamikazes. Three were shot down, but one hit LCI(G)-70, a landing craft turned gunship escorting the minesweepers.

Three days before the landings on January 6, the Japanese threw 60 kamikazes at the Allies in Lingayen Gulf, including 20 twin-engine aircraft. This was everything they could scrape together, including four G4Ms, one of only two occasions the type would be committed as kamikazes. They struck and damaged a dozen ships, and sank another.

Two battleships, the *New Mexico* and *California*, were hit. Both suffered casualties exceeding 100, but neither was damaged enough to pause operations. The *Louisville* and *Australia* were both hit again, as was the light cruiser *Columbia*. *Louisville*'s damage was so bad it had to withdraw from the gun line supporting troops ashore. Four destroyers were also damaged over the course of the day, as were two fast transports, converted from

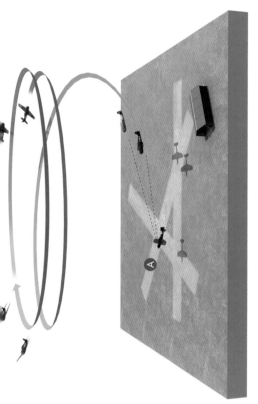

1. While TF 38 cruised east of Luzon, it launched patrols over all of Luzon's Japanese airfields, large and small, launching and recovering aircraft as necessary to provide continuous coverage of each.

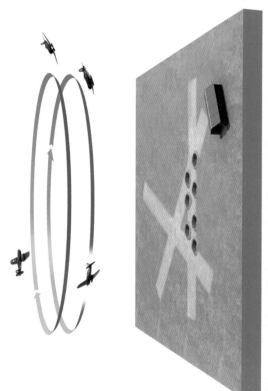

2. US carrier aircraft circle a Japanese airfield. Whenever a Japanese aircraft attempts to launch from that field (A), some of the patrolling aircraft drop out of the coverage to shoot the plane down as it is taking off.

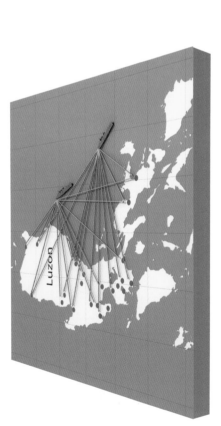

3. As the original patrol runs out of fuel, it has to return to the carrier to refuel and rearm. (A) During the gap in fighter coverage, carrier bombers (either Avengers or Helldivers) bomb and strafe the airfield, preventing Japanese aircraft from launching (B). Meanwhile a relief fighter patrol arrives over the airfield.

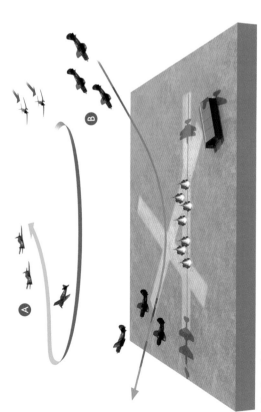

4. Upon completion of the bomber attack, the new fighter patrol takes up station over the enemy airfield, again awaiting any Japanese attempts to launch aircraft.

A corpsman treats a casualty, a sailor who suffered burns as a result of a kamikaze strike during the invasion at Lingayen Gulf. Gasoline carried by kamikazes frequently caused more damage than their bombs. (AC)

old flush-deck destroyers. Finally, USS *Southard*, another old flush-decker converted to a minesweeper, was sunk.

Casualties in these strikes were high for two reasons. Firstly, due to invasion preparation strikes on the intended landing sites, the escort carriers could only allocate 24 fighters for CAP at any time. These were Wildcats, which were inferior to some of the aircraft used as kamikazes. Furthermore, poor weather prevented TF38, east of Luzon, from blanketing Luzon's airfields on January 6.

TF38 had returned to sea on December 28, 1944, to suppress Japanese kamikaze activities prior to the Lingayen landings. On January 3, it struck Formosa airfields, spending two successful days working them over. Strikes destroyed an estimated 100 Japanese aircraft, including many kamikazes. Consequently, no aircraft from Formosa successfully attacked ships in Lingayen Gulf over the next week. TF38 turned its attention to Luzon on January 6, only to be frustrated by bad weather over the carriers and Luzon airfields. It did shoot down 32 Japanese aircraft, but the rest leaked through to Lingayen.

TF38 was more successful on January 7. Despite continued foul weather, and assisted by USAAF aircraft from Mindoro, it kept Japanese air forces in Luzon largely grounded. Carrier aircraft shot down four Japanese planes and destroyed an estimated 75 more on the ground. No kamikazes struck Lingayen that day. TF38 refueled on January 8 and turned its attentions back to Formosa on January 9, ensuring no aircraft from there could interfere with that day's landing operations.

The task force's departure permitted resumption of kamikaze activities in the Philippines, albeit at much lower levels than previously. Most of the Japanese air forces in the Philippines had been destroyed, and no reinforcements had arrived. Despite that, the IJA launched 11 single-engine and four Ki-45 kamikazes and the IJN one B6N kamikaze on January 8. They hit the *Australia* again and damaged the escort carriers *Kitkun Bay* and *Kadashan Bay* badly enough that both had to retire for repairs. Additionally, an LST in a supply convoy in the Surigao Strait, headed for Lingayen, was slightly damaged by a kamikaze.

The IJA and IJN sent five kamikaze aircraft each against the invasion force on January 9, and the Army seven on January 10, 27 on January 12, and two on January 13. Most of the IJA aircraft were twin-engine types, except for 22 Ki-84s sent out on January 12. The Ki-84 was a front-line fighter, previously little used for kamikaze duties. Thereafter, kamikaze activities in the Philippines ceased, as both services pulled their surviving aircraft out of the theater.

The bag for the Japanese for that final week was unimpressive: no ships were sunk, with 17 damaged. The unlucky *Australia* and *Colombia* were hit again, this time badly enough to send both back for major refits, as was the escort carrier *Salamaua*. The battleship *Mississippi* was moderately damaged, but remained on station. One destroyer, four destroyer escorts, seven transports or cargo ships, and one LST made up the rest of the damaged ships. They represented a trivial fraction of the nearly 900 Allied vessels which participated in the invasion.

Combat air patrols at Lingayen Gulf were largely conducted by escort carrier groups, carrying F4F or FM2 Wildcats. While the Wildcat was superior to the aircraft kamikazes flew, they were not as capable as the first-line Hellcat and Corsair. This allowed more kamikazes to get through. (AC)

## Formosa, Iwo Jima, and long-range raids: January 14–March 26, 1945

Japan's air forces abandoned the Philippines after it became apparent the Allied invasion of Luzon would succeed. The action around the Philippines was a real body blow for the kamikaze force, which expended many of its experienced volunteers, forcing the use of less-trained pilots. Worse still, the Allies appeared to have developed successful countermeasures. For while they could not stop all kamikazes, they could significantly reduce their effectiveness. Yet kamikazes still seemed the most effective way to attack the Allies, so the campaign continued and was even expanded.

The kamikaze program's expansion was not geographical, however. While the IJA committed some kamikazes to defend holdings in Southeast Asia and the Dutch East Indies against British advances there, only a small number were used. Most were drawn from locally available aircraft. The campaign's focus remained the defense of the Home Islands. Kamikazes were deployed where they could best delay any Allied advance, which in the short term meant the Bonin Islands or possibly Formosa. The Japanese air forces stocked both sets of islands with kamikazes, leaving other areas largely bare of them.

Meanwhile, the Allies were expanding the policies which succeeded for them in the Philippines. Before TF38 departed Ulithi on December 28, 1944, it increased the number of fighters carried by its fleet carriers. Two Marine Corps F4U squadrons were added, with Helldivers eliminated on two carriers: USS *Essex* and USS *Wasp* left Ulithi carrying 91 fighters and 15 TBD torpedo bombers. Additionally, TF38.5, a "fifth" carrier task group, was organized on January 5, consisting of the night operations carriers *Enterprise* and *Independence* and six destroyers. It operated within TG38.2 during the day to concentrate CAP and antiaircraft protection, breaking off to conduct night operations.

After January 9, TF38 ended support of the Lingayen landings to conduct a two-week raid on Japanese shipping and aircraft in and around the South China Sea. They were largely untroubled by kamikazes during the raid, as there were no kamikazes covering the South

The fast carriers missed Lingayen Gulf because they were raiding the South China Sea. The raid hit areas without *tokko* units, but its ships ended up attacked by kamikazes as they left. A kamikaze is shown hitting the *Ticonderoga* after raids on eastern Formosa. (AC)

China Sea. However, Japan did have kamikazes stationed at bases on Formosa's south coast as an invasion reaction force.

Trouble began for TF38 upon exiting the South China Sea. On January 20, it launched a series of airstrikes against Formosa to destroy aircraft missed during earlier sweeps. TF38 avoided kamikazes during the two earlier airstrikes made against Formosa airfields during the sweep. One launched at the beginning had the advantage of surprise. The second was launched inside the South China Sea, hitting from a direction unprotected by kamikazes. The carrier attacks planned for January 21 found TF38 100 miles east of Formosa's southern coast, where Japan had kamikazes within reach of the task force in both Formosa and Luzon (possibly the last flyable aircraft on Luzon). Three waves of kamikazes struck the task force in an all-IJN attack. Except for minor kamikaze attacks on the British in the East Indies, the IJA had retired from *tokko* missions to prepare for the defense of Japan.

The attacks began shortly after noon, when seven aircraft – four kamikazes and three escorts – approached TG38.3 from Formosa. At 1206hrs, a lone aircraft targeted the light carrier *Langley* and dropped two bombs, one of which hit the flight deck and ripped a 10ftx14ft hole in the deck, starting small fires. At 1208hrs, a kamikaze dived at and hit the *Ticonderoga*. Its bomb penetrated and exploded above the hangar deck, setting aircraft fueled and armed for flight on fire. The subsequent fires spread deep into the ship before being brought under control.

Almost simultaneously, TG38.2 was attacked by seven kamikazes and their six escorts, which launched from Tuguegarao in Luzon. CAP fighters were vectored to the bandits, intercepting them before they reached the ships and breaking up the attack. The aircraft not shot down by the intercepting Hellcats retired.

Another 13 aircraft from Formosa, with eight kamikazes, launched a fresh attack on TG38.3 at 1250hrs. Six kamikazes were intercepted and shot down, but the surviving pair dived on the damaged *Ticonderoga*. One was shot down, but the second crashed into *Ticonderoga*'s island superstructure, engulfing it and the surrounding flight deck with blazing gasoline. It took 90 minutes to bring all the fires under control. The *Ticonderoga* lost 143 crew killed in this action, with 202 wounded and 36 aircraft destroyed.

A further attack struck the picket destroyer *Maddox*. A Zero slipped in with US aircraft returning to the carriers. The Tom Cat destroyer failed to detect the Zero, which peeled off and dived at the *Maddox*, crashing amidships. The Allen M. Sumner-class destroyer, which had seven crew killed and 33 wounded, suffered moderate damage but survived to serve again, most notably as one of the principal ships in the Vietnam War's Gulf of Tonkin incident.

Thereafter, matters went into hiatus for several weeks. The Japanese lacked opportunities to strike at Allied fleets after TF38's sweep into the South China Sea. TF38 returned to Ulithi on January 25, where it would remain for the next three weeks. The Third Fleet became the Fifth Fleet on January 26 and began preparing for the invasion of Iwo Jima, scheduled for mid-February. The Japanese, although they realized the kamikazes could not stop the Allies, were expanding the kamikaze corps, regardless. But they were beginning to exhaust their pool of trained pilots for *tokko* duty and were having to turn instead to student pilots.

The Fifth Fleet left Ulithi on February 10 to support the Iwo Jima landings. The slower escort carrier group, TG52.2, steamed almost directly towards Iwo Jima, making a dogleg to Guam and Saipan before arriving at Iwo Jima on February 16. TF58 reached the Bonin Islands on February 17, but steamed north to Honshu, launching airstrikes in Tokyo Bay on February 16 and the following morning before scooting back to support the landings.

The two days of Tokyo air raids garnered no kamikaze attacks in response. There were no *tokko* units around Tokyo, and none could be organized before the Fast Carrier Task Force withdrew. Similarly, there was no kamikaze response at Iwo Jima between the arrival of the Allied fleet and the day after the landings. There were none available within the Bonin Islands.

Allied forces neutralized most of the kamikaze threat at Iwo Jima by attacking every airfield on and around the island. The results of pre-invasion airstrikes on one Iwo Jima airfield are shown here. (AC)

One lesson the Allies learned during the clashes in the Philippines was that the best way to prevent kamikaze attacks was to prevent them from taking off. At Iwo Jima it was easier to blanket the area than it had been at the Philippines. The Bonin Islands were smaller geographically, with much less land area available for airfields. It was also within range of long-range US bombers based in the Marianas. It was not only within range of the B-29s hitting Japan, it could also be reached by B-24s escorted by long-range fighters. These saturated the Bonin airfields, bombing runways and facilities, strafing aircraft on the ground, and shooting down any that took off. Well before the Fifth Fleet's arrival, Iwo Jima's airfields were smashed, logistical and maintenance facilities flattened, runways cratered, and aircraft destroyed.

Finally, the Fifth Fleet announced its arrival with an intense period of bombardment. All of Iwo Jima's airfields were within range of naval gunfire, as well as aircraft. The escort carriers' Wildcats were numerous enough to seal off the skies above the island during the pre-landing

Kamikaze strikes at Iwo Jima were limited to missions originating in Japan. Despite the 800nmi range, these strikes did some damage. The crew of the *Saratoga* are shown fighting fires caused in the aftermath of attacks made by two waves of kamikazes. (AC)

bombardment, and once the fast carriers arrived by the afternoon of February 17, the US Navy had air supremacy over the Bonins.

To oppose the Allies, Japan initially launched conventional airstrikes from Honshu. The aircraft took off from the IJN's Hatori airfield near Yokosuka, refueling at Hachijo Jima's airfields midway between Honshu and Iwo Jima. The first attacks were made during the night of February 20/21. The US counted 13 separate attacks comprising a total of 18–20 aircraft. These attacks yielded no hits. The escort carriers lacked night-operations equipped fighters, so the *Saratoga* was sent to protect the escort carrier group; along with the *Enterprise*, it was one of two night operations aircraft carriers.

On February 21, a new *tokko*, the *Mitate* unit, was organized and sent to strike at the Fifth Fleet. The first wave of these kamikazes arrived in the afternoon, just as the *Saratoga* reached its new patrol station northwest of Iwo Jima. Caught on radar 75 miles out, the incoming Japanese were initially identified as "friendly." Fighters from *Saratoga*'s CAP were sent to investigate. A 1650hrs they discovered that the "friendlies" were bandits and attacked them, shooting down two Zeros escorting the kamikazes. The *Saratoga*, with most of its planes aboard, began launching night fighters. At 1659hrs, six kamikazes dived out of the clouds at the *Saratoga* from 3,500ft.

Five of the kamikazes damaged the *Saratoga*, but the sixth missed. Two landed in the water and bounced into the *Saratoga*'s waterline, their bombs striking the carrier and exploding. A third plane exploded on the anchor windlass, destroying part of the forward flight deck. A fourth exploded after hitting the port catapult, while the fifth hit a starboard aircraft crane. Already blazing, the latter aircraft broke apart, with pieces landing on the forward gun gallery while the rest of the wreck fell harmlessly into the sea.

The whole attack lasted just three minutes. All the damage was topside, with the ship's machinery spaces undamaged. The fires were doused by 1845hrs, and damage control had the situation in hand. A few minutes later, a second kamikaze strike targeted the *Saratoga*, with five aircraft diving down on the old carrier. Four were shot down, but the fifth hit, its bomb blowing a 25ft hole in the flight deck but the gasoline-filled airplane bounced overboard.

Damage control got the fresh damage under control within an hour, but the forward flight deck was now unusable. Regardless, by 2015hrs the *Saratoga* was recovering aircraft on the aft flight deck. The attacks cost the *Saratoga* 123 crew killed and 192 wounded, with 42 aircraft lost – 36 burned or jettisoned and six forced to ditch when unable to land. Spruance, the Fifth Fleet commander, ordered the carrier stateside for repairs. It steamed to the West Coast under its own power, returning to service four months later as a training carrier.

The *Saratoga* was not the second strike's only victim. At 1645hrs, escort carrier USS *Bismarck Sea* was attacked. Although it shot down one kamikaze, a second low-flying kamikaze flew into its starboard side, striking abreast of its aft elevator. It is believed that the kamikaze's bomb, cooking off in the burning wreckage, exploded two minutes later, setting ablaze fueled hangar deck aircraft. Within 20 minutes, the fires were out of control. The *Bismarck Sea* was abandoned at 1905hrs and sank three hours later.

Simultaneously, four torpedo bombers attacked another escort carrier in the group, USS *Lunga Point*. Three of the bombers attempted to crash

Escort carrier *Lunga Point* was luckier than the *Saratoga* or sister escort carrier *Bismarck Sea*. Although theses flames look spectacular, the burning B5N they came from skidded over the *Lunga Point*'s flight deck and into the ocean on the other side. (AC)

# The Iwo Jima attack

On February 21, 1945, a 51-aircraft strike, including kamikazes, was launched from Japan. The aircraft refueled at Hachijō-jima, with 31 reaching Iwo Jima. The attack sank the escort carrier *Bismarck Sea*, and damaged escort carrier *Lunga Point*, fleet carrier *Saratoga*, a net cargo ship, and two LSTs.

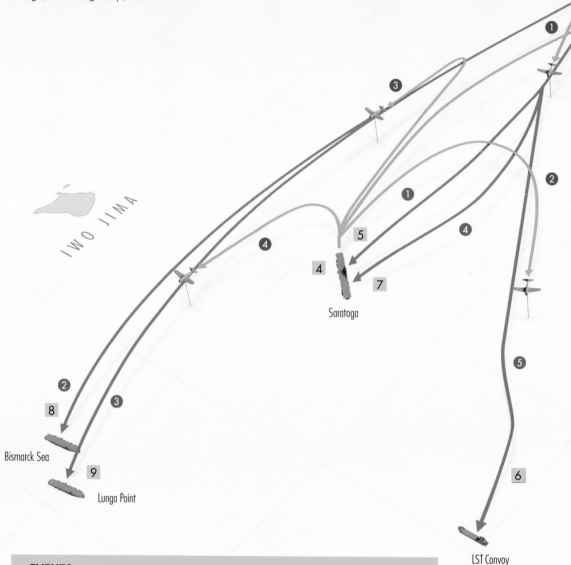

IWO JIMA

Saratoga

Bismarck Sea

Lunga Point

LST Convoy

## EVENTS

1. 1000 – Japanese aircraft depart Hatori Airfield near Yokohama.

2. 1200 – Japanese aircraft depart Hachijō-jima after refueling.

3. 1628 – Bogies (Japanese aircraft) spotted incoming by *Saratoga*'s radar.

4. 1630–1659 – *Saratoga* launches 21 F6F fighters.

5. 1700–1703 – Six kamikazes dive on *Saratoga*, five hit *Saratoga*.

6. 1720 – Four D4Ys attack an LST convoy, hitting net tender *Keokuk* and LST-477.

7. 1846 – Five more kamikazes attack *Saratoga*, four are shot down, one hits.

8. 1846 – A kamikaze strikes *Bismarck Sea*. Fires started by the hit force the ship to be abandoned.

9. 1850 – Four torpedo bombers attack *Lunga Point*. All miss, but one skids over the flight deck causing minor fires.

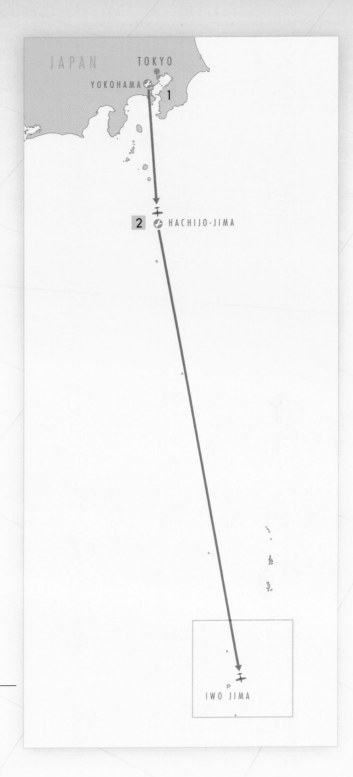

**Japanese Units:**

1. 310th FS/1 (six A6M)
2. 1st AS/1 (six B5N)
3. 1st AS/1 (six B5N)
4. 254th AS/1 (six D4Y)
5. 254th AS/2 (four D4Y)

**US Units:** ●

1. CAG(N)-53/1 (six F6F)
2. CAG(N)-53/2 (four F6F)
3. CAG(N)-53/3 (four F6F)
4. CAG(N)-53/4 (four F6F)

Japan launched a long-distance kamikaze strike against Ulithi on March 10, 1945. Twenty-four P1Y Ginga bombers, like those in this picture, left Japan for the Fifth Fleet anchorage, where TF58 was present. Only two Gingas reached Ulithi and just one hit a carrier. (AC)

into the carrier after dropping their torpedoes. All the torpedoes missed and two of the spontaneous kamikazes were shot down, but the remaining one struck *Lunga Point*'s island. The plane slewed along the flight deck before its momentum took it overboard. The *Lunga Point* suffered only minor damage, quickly quenched the fires, and was back on duty within an hour.

A third kamikaze attack struck an LST group southeast of Iwo Jima at 1720hrs that evening. Net cargo ship *Keokuk*, a converted train ferry launched in 1918, was struck just behind the starboard bridge by a B6N torpedo bomber which dived out of the clouds from ahead of the ship. The airplane scraped down the starboard side before going overboard. It destroyed most of the 20mm guns in the aft starboard battery, killing 17 crew and wounding 44. The *Keokuk*, too, was quickly able to resume its duties. A second kamikaze struck LST-477, without doing serious damage to it or its cargo of tanks.

Except for a lone kamikaze on March 1, which was shot down without doing damage, February 21 ended the kamikaze campaign at Iwo Jima. The attacking aircraft were all single-engine IJN carrier aircraft. Those that dived at the Allied ships were radar-equipped bombers, which would explain why attacks concentrated on the *Saratoga*: it was the largest blip on the screen.

On March 10, the IJN launched its first – and only – long-range strategic *tokko* strike of the war, an attack on the US Navy's Ulithi anchorage intended to cripple the Fast Carrier Task Force. The operation was called *Second Tansaku*, or *Tan #2*. (*Tan #1* was a similar but cancelled plan for a non-kamikaze Ulithi airstrike during the summer of 1944.) Planning for *Tan #2* had begun in early February.

Ulithi was within one-way range of Kyushu for an armed P1Y Ginga. The plan required the Fifth Fleet to be at Ulithi for it to succeed, however. Once past the point of no return, the Ginga could not fly back to base, and the attack would be wasted if the anchorage was empty. Pre-mission reconnaissance was therefore essential.

On February 14, 24 Gingas from the 762nd Naval Air Group were reconstituted as the Azusa Special Attack Unit. Each was armed with an 800kg demolition bomb. Due to the extreme range and concerns about the pilots' navigation skills, three four-engine Kawanishi H8K flying boats were assigned as pathfinder aircraft to guide the bombers. Four other bombers were to conduct weather reconnaissance along the route.

To conduct pre-mission scouting, seven long-range C6N Saiuns – single-engine reconnaissance aircraft – were sent to Truk from Japan on February 11. Just two of them arrived at Truk, but one was damaged while landing. The sole flyable aircraft made its first overflight of Ulithi on February 13, discovering the anchorage empty: the Fifth Fleet had departed for Iwo Jima. The mission was duly postponed until early March.

On March 5, reconnaissance flights resumed. That day's flight discovered 16 carriers at Ulithi. A flight on March 9 identified six fleet, three light, and seven escort carriers at Ulithi, with four other "unidentified" carriers also present. The report was sent to Tokyo the following day, and Admiral Ukagi scheduled the strike for March 11.

However, things went wrong from the start. The weather aircraft departed late, as did some of the pathfinder H8Ks. Of the 24 P1Ys that left Kanoya airfield in Kyushu at 0920hrs, six soon returned due to engine problems. One of the pathfinders also disappeared. The remaining P1Ys encountered headwinds and rain squalls, burning more fuel than expected. Additional Gingas developed mechanical problems and were forced to land at Japanese-held islands, while two ditched at sea when their fuel ran out.

One group descended from the clouds when they thought they were near Ulithi to discover a navigation error had left them near Japanese-held Yap, 100nmi west of Ulithi. By then they lacked the fuel to reach Ulithi, so they had to land at Yap. However, Yap lacked fuel, so those aircraft were now stuck. Two P1Ys reached Ulithi over an hour after sunset. They flew into the atoll undetected, with no alert sounded. The islands and ships were lit up, many of the crews watching movies.

One P1Y smashed into USS *Randolph*, an Essex-class carrier, hitting it just below the flight deck. The Ginga was so low on gasoline it failed to catch fire, but its bomb exploded between the flight deck and hangar deck, causing significant damage. Casualties numbered 26 dead and 105 wounded. The other Ginga's pilot somehow mistook a lighted athletic field at Mog Mog Island for an aircraft carrier, and crashed his bomber into a baseball diamond. The *Randolph* would be repaired at Ulithi, returning to duty on April 7.

# The long grind, Okinawa: March 27–June 30, 1945

After the conquest of the Bonins, attention turned to the Ryukyu Islands, the logical next step towards invading the Japanese Home Islands. The Bonins were too small and too far from the Home Islands to support an invasion. However, the central islands in the Ryukyus – known as the Okinawa Gunto (group) – contained large islands with good harbors. These islands – including the largest, Okinawa – were within fighter range of Kyushu. Both sides knew this and planned accordingly.

USS *Halsey Powell* after being hit by a kamikaze on March 21, 1945. It was attacked as part of an unsuccessful Japanese attempt to destroy the Fast Carrier Task Force as it attacked Japan's Home Islands. The Fletcher-class destroyer was not even the target, being hit by a kamikaze that missed the fleet carrier *Hancock*. (AC)

## **OPPOSITE** KAMIKAZE ATTACKS IN OKINAWA

The Allies' plan, Operation *Iceberg*, envisioned taking the islands and their airfields; first Okinawa, with five airfields, and then Ie Shima, on its northwest side, with its additional airfield. Okinawa, the region's administrative capital, also had two outstanding harbors which could host a massive fleet for the invasion of Kyushu.

The Allies intended first to take the Kerama Rhetto to support the Okinawa invasion. These small, rocky islands west of Okinawa's southern end were too small for airfields, but were lightly held. They offered a sheltered anchorage for kamikaze-damaged ships, something Iwo Jima showed was necessary. The Allied invasion of Okinawa was scheduled for April 1, with the Kerama Retto landings preceding those by a week.

The Japanese planned a bloody, delaying ground action in the island's southern half, before retiring to its mountainous north. In the air, they planned Operation *Ten-Go*, a massive 2,000-plane strike with both conventional and kamikaze aircraft by April 1. Japan consequently ramped up kamikaze training, and placed all kamikazes – Army and Navy – under the command of Admiral Ugaki. Airfields in Okinawa were abandoned, with the kamikazes striking from Kyushu and Formosa.

The Allies opened the campaign with pre-invasion airstrikes at airfields from which Japan could launch kamikazes – in Kyushu, the Ryukyus, and Formosa. TF58 sortied from Ulithi on March 14 to strike Kyushu and the Okinawa Gunto. Strikes on Kyushu commenced on March 16. The battle continued through three days of carrier strikes on Kyushu and the Inland Sea, with two days of Japanese counterstrikes on the withdrawing carriers.

The Japanese grabbed the opportunity to attempt to destroy the Fast Carrier Task Force, attacking TF58 with 193 aircraft. This included the first combat use of the Ohka on March 21, but they failed to register any hits, the bombers carrying them being attacked and driven off. By the time the six-day fight ended, the Japanese had lost 161

The first operational use of the Ohka flying bomb was on March 21, 1945. With its short range, it had to be carried close to its target by a carrier aircraft, typically a G4M bomber. On March 21, US fighter cover shot down all the mother bombers before they came close enough to launch their Ohkas. (AC)

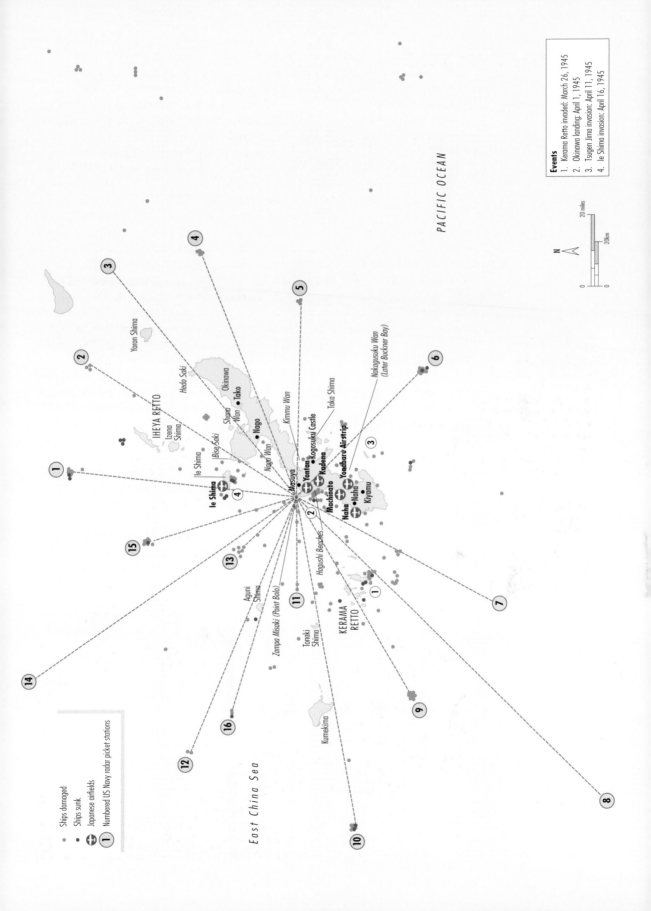

**PACIFIC OCEAN**

**East China Sea**

IHEYA RETTO

Yoron Shima

Izena Shima

Hedo Saki

Okinawa

Iheya

Shuri Wan

Ie Shima

Bise-Saki

Nago Wan

Nago

Taka

Kimmu Wan

Motobu

Yontan

Kagosuku Castle

Kadena

Toka Shima

Yonabaru Airstrip

Machinato

Naha

Naha

Kiyamu

Nakagusuku Wan
(Later Buckner Bay)

Zampa Misaki (Point Bolo)

Aguni Shima

Hagushi Beaches

Tonaki Shima

KERAMA RETTO

Kumekima

Ships damaged

Ships sunk

Japanese airfields

Numbered US Navy radar picket stations

**Events**
1. Kerama Retto invaded: March 26, 1945
2. Okinawa landing: April 1, 1945
3. Tsugen Jima invasion: April 11, 1945
4. Ie Shima invasion: April 16, 1945

N

0    20 miles
0    20km

aircraft in the air. They lost several hundred more on the ground from carrier airstrikes. In exchange, they damaged the fleet carriers *Franklin*, *Yorktown*, and *Enterprise* and the destroyer *Halsey Powell*. The latter was collateral damage, hit by a kamikaze that missed the carrier *Hancock*.

The *Yorktown* and *Enterprise* were back in action by April 5; *Halsey Powell* by August. However, USS *Franklin* was out of the war, as it took a month for the carrier to reach Brooklyn Navy Yard for repairs, which were not completed until June 1946. The *Franklin* suffered 724 crew killed and 265 wounded, mostly due to fires aboard. Ironically, it was damaged by conventional bombing, not a kamikaze.

The southern Ryukyus and Formosa were covered by TF57, made up of ships from the British Pacific Fleet. It consisted of four fleet carriers, two King George V-class battleships, five light cruisers, and 15 destroyers. Supported by a service squadron of tankers, repair ships, and escort carriers carrying replacement aircraft, it operated within the Fifth Fleet independently of the US TF58, arriving at Ulithi on March 20.

As the Okinawa campaign opened, TF57's first task was covering Sakishima Gunto. Strung out between Okinawa and Formosa, these were the southernmost islands in the Ryukyus. TF57 arrived on station late on March 25. Beginning after dawn on March 26, the British started two days of airstrikes on Miyako Retto, Sakishima Gunto's easternmost island. Only 186 miles from Okinawa, its airfields threatened any Okinawa invasion, offering a base from which aircraft from Formosa could stage and operate.

After neutralizing the airfields, TF57 withdrew to refuel. During its absence, one of two seven-carrier escort carrier strike groups assigned to support the Okinawa landings covered Sakishima Gunto. TF57 returned on March 30, relieving the escort carriers for invasion-day duties. Meanwhile, the British kept the southern approaches to Okinawa closed to Japanese aircraft over the critical period from March 30 to April 2.

Operation *Iceberg* ground into action on March 24, when the minesweepers first arrived off Kerama Retto, the vanguard of 1,300 ships supporting the 155,000 Allied troops to be landed. On March 26, an infantry division landed at Kerama Retto, quickly capturing five of its largest islands in simultaneous landings. On April 1, four infantry divisions – two US Army and two US Marine Corps – landed on Okinawa.

During this period, TF58 guarded the approaches to Okinawa from Japanese aircraft from Kyushu while TF57 watched the southern flank. The escort carriers of TG52.1, the Support Carrier Group, provided close air support for the invading troops. They also provided CAP over the invasion fleet and used any other available aircraft to blanket Japanese airfields on Okinawa and Ie Shima.

The Japanese reaction was the last thing expected by the Allies. They mounted no opposition to the landings, the Japanese defenders waiting inland to engage the Allied infantry beyond the range of naval gunfire support. Even more surprising was the lack of enemy aircraft. A swarm of kamikazes had been expected to oppose the landings. Instead, between March 24 and April 5, there were persistent, low-level kamikaze attacks by only small groups of aircraft.

Yet these attacks were significant, the Allied fleet hit by just over 200 kamikazes during that period. Between March 24 and 31, an average of seven kamikazes struck each day. On April 1, the day of the main landing, and the two days following, between 40 and 60 kamikazes attacked. The next two days saw a reversion to the earlier pattern, with one kamikaze sent on April 4 and ten on April 5.

During operations to take Kerama Retto, 11 ships were hit by kamikazes. Most of these were destroyers or smaller, but they included the battleship *Nevada* and light cruiser *Biloxi*. USS *Nevada* took moderate damage, having a turret temporarily knocked out. Two destroyers and a destroyer escort suffered significant damage, the remaining ships receiving only light damage.

During and immediately after the initial Okinawa landings, from March 31 to April 4, a further 18 ships were struck off Okinawa, with another kamikaze hitting HMS *Indefatigable*, one of the carriers in TF57. Besides *Indefatigable*, three major US warships were hit: the battleship *West Virginia*, heavy cruiser *Indianapolis*, and escort carrier *Wake Island*. The remaining casualties were a variety of invasion ships and small escort warships: 11 cargo ships or amphibious warfare ships and three destroyers or destroyers converted to auxiliary duties.

None of these ships were sunk, although two – LST-884 and the *Dickerson*, an old flush-deck destroyer converted to a fast transport – were later scuttled after surveys showed them so badly damaged as to be not worth repairing. The major warships suffered only light to moderate damage. Three transports, including a converted destroyer, took damage severe enough to require most of the rest of the war to repair. The rest of the transports received moderate to light damage from kamikazes.

The total number of kamikazes sent each day was similar to what was seen during operations in the Philippines. But although the number of kamikaze sorties during the first three days of the Okinawa landings matched the scale seen at the Lingayen landings, their effectiveness seemed a lot lower to the Allies. The Okinawa kamikaze pilots were less skilled than their predecessors, and were thus proving easier to intercept and shoot down.

The kamikazes were also were being intercepted earlier and more skillfully than previously. After Iwo Jima, Spruance and his staff developed a far more extensive early warning and interception system. Sixteen radar picket stations ringed Okinawa, continuously occupied by one or two radar-equipped destroyers or destroyer escorts. These were positioned anywhere from 18–95nmi from the tip of Zampa Misaki (designated "Point Bolo" by the Allies), just

# Scratch one more kamikaze

On March 21, 1945, Japan unleashed the Yokosuka MXY-7 Ohka rocket bomb on the US Fifth Fleet. TF58 was conducting a series of raids on Japan's Home Islands, so in retaliation, Ohkas were sent against the US ships.

Yet the Ohkas never reached the fleet. They had only a short range – 20 nautical miles – and had to be carried to their target by twin-engine bombers, generally the Mitsubishi G4M (code named "Betty" by the Allies and dubbed the "Type 1 cigarette lighter" by their crews for their propensity to catch fire when hit). The G4Ms were intercepted by US Navy fighters 50 miles from the US carriers.

It was a US fighter pilot's dream. The fast-flying G4Ms were slowed and their maneuverability crippled by their cargo of Ohkas. The bombers' escort was down to 30 fighters and they were too high to interfere with the Hellcats from CV-18 (*Hornet*) as they attacked. The Red Five division of *Hornet*'s VF-17 ("Jolly Rogers") was led by Lieutenant James "Jim" L. Pearce, with his wingman George Johnson. They attacked the formation from the right, while Lieutenant "Hal" Mitchell's Red Twenty-Eight division attacked from the left.

Pearce quickly shot down one G4M, the formation's flight leader, following it down to look at its Ohka. After the bomber exploded, Pearce returned to the formation for a second run, pictured here.

This time he approached from behind and the right. When the tail gunner began shooting at him, Pearce hosed the tail with .50cal fire, killing the gunner. Then he shifted his aim to a wing, between the wing and engine nacelles. His bullets ignited the gasoline tank there, setting the wing ablaze. With the wing engulfed in flames, either the bomber's pilot released the Ohka or the Ohka pilot decided it was time to leave. The manned bomb fell free from the blazing bomber and headed towards the ocean. It was soon joined by the G4M.

After Pearce finished off his second G4M, he looked around to discover "Bettys flaming all over the sky." There were no more for him to target. None of the G4Ms got close enough to *Hornet*'s TG58.1 for the Ohkas they were carrying to attack the formation. All were shot down.

The effort achieved nothing for Japan, and cost them 18 irreplaceable G4Ms and 15 MXY-7s, along with the crews. It reduced the force available for the *kikusui* attack planned as a response to the anticipated Allied invasion of Okinawa, which occurred 12 days later. Japan would not mount another Ohka attack until April 16.

Pearce ended his day with two kills. In all, he would be credited with five-and-a-quarter aircraft shot down during World War II (the fractional kill was a shared credit). He survived the war, became a Navy test pilot after the war, and went on to a long career with North American Aviation as both a test pilot and a manager in the Apollo Program which put man on the moon.

north of the initial landing beaches on Okinawa. This radar ring provided the invasion fleet off the beaches with almost two hours' warning of incoming enemy air strikes.

"Point Bolo" offered a convenient location for aerial overwatch of the invasion's Hagushi beaches. Fighters stationed there were dispatched to intercept bogies detected by the radar pickets. Between the start of the Kerama Retto landings and the end of April 5, the situation worked well. The British sealed off the southern approaches, the radar pickets provided sufficient warning of air raids approaching from Japan, and fighter cover successfully intercepted most of the bandits before they reached the invasion ships. Some were even beginning to believe the kamikazes were beaten, or at least that their threat had been contained.

The next day, Admiral Ugaki activated Operation *Ten-Go*, the Japanese counteroffensive. Primarily a naval effort, including a final sortie by the IJN's surface ships, it included an aerial component supported jointly by both services' air forces. Called *kikusui* (floating chrysanthemum), each raid included both conventional and suicide aircraft. Each *kikusui* wave was numbered, with ultimately ten two-day waves being sent.

*Kikusui* 1, which began on April 6, was the largest, involving nearly 700 aircraft over two days, including 355 kamikazes. Although the most massive of the ten waves, it was far less than what had been planned and was executed nearly a week late. Many aircraft intended for *Kikusui* 1 were lost due to TF38's late-March Kyushu airstrikes, which delayed the wave until replacements were found. Yet even at half its intended strength, it was horrific.

It began in the pre-dawn hours of April 6, when radar at Picket Stations 1 and 2 picked up incoming aircraft. The strikes continued intermittently until well after dark on April 7. Twenty-three ships were hit on April 6, more than in the previous seven days combined, with a further eight hit the following day.

Nearly a quarter of the *Kikusui* 1 kamikazes were expended attacking destroyers assigned to Picket Stations 1–3. Attacks began at 0230hrs and continued until well into the afternoon. Before midnight, both destroyers originally assigned to Station 1 and 2, the *Colhoun* and *Bush*, sank due to accumulated damage. More destroyers were sent to rescue survivors and maintain the radar watch.

The escort carrier crews called Kerama Retto "Kamikaze Corner." The *Sangamon*, present with the Taffy 1 escort carrier group in the Philippines, gets a return visit from a kamikaze off Okinawa on May 4. The aircraft missed the *Sangamon* by only 25ft. (AC)

The only good news about the concentration on the three picket destroyers was that it left fewer kamikazes to hit the rest of the Allied fleet. But there were still plenty of kamikazes left, over four times the number that had been sent on any previous day. Swarms of kamikazes rained down on six different ship concentrations in Okinawa and its surrounding waters. These included shipping in and around Kerama Retto, transports and cargo ships unloading off the Hagushi beaches, a battleship gunfire support unit off Ie Shima, destroyers in the antisubmarine screen south of Okinawa, a group of destroyers on antisubmarine patrol east of Okinawa, antiaircraft pickets guarding approaches to the beachhead west of Okinawa, and the Fast Carrier Task Force, then 100nmi northeast of the beachhead.

The Kerama Retto attack sank the only other ship lost that day, the ammunition ship *Hobbs Victory*. *Logan Victory*, another ammunition ship there, was also hit, but only damaged. *LST-447*, approaching Kerama Retto after discharging its cargo at Hashigushi, was hit too, sinking the next day. The light carrier *San Jacinto*, with TF38, was slightly damaged by a kamikaze's near miss. Eight more destroyers, two destroyer escorts, seven

minesweepers, and two LSTs were damaged by kamikazes that day, several severely enough to keep them out of action until the war's end.

Attacks continued the following day, but at a lighter rate. Seven ships were hit, with the destroyer-minesweeper *Emmons* sunk. Other ships hit that day included USS *Maryland* (part of the battleship screen protecting the transports from a potential attack by the giant Japanese battleship *Yamato*) and the fleet carrier *Hancock* (with TF38 hunting and sinking the *Yamato*). *Maryland*'s damage was too minor to cause it to leave station, but the *Hancock* was kept out of combat until the end of June. Two destroyers, a destroyer escort, and a minesweeper were also struck.

While *Kikusui* 1 inflicted impressive casualties, the Allies felt they had the situation in hand. On April 7, Admiral Richard Kelly Turner, commanding the invasion fleet, signaled Pearl Harbor, "If this is the best the enemy can throw against us, we shall prevail." The next day, after *Yamato*'s sinking, he sent a message to Chester Nimitz, Commander-in-Chief Pacific Fleet, saying, "I may be crazy, but it looks like the Japanese have quit the war, at least in this sector." Nimitz replied, "Delete all after 'crazy.'"

Adjustments made by the Allies after the attacks included increasing the destroyers at each radar picket station from one to two, and adding up to three amphibious warfare ships – typically medium landing ships (LSMs) or large support landing craft (LCS(L)s) – to increase antiaircraft defenses, help with damage control, and provide rescue when necessary. Additionally, CAP over the radar picket stations was improved.

Two dozen independent kamikazes, operating in small numbers, attacked in the days following the end of *Kikusui* 1. These concentrated on ships at Picket Stations 1–4, north of Okinawa. Between April 8 and 11, they damaged three destroyers and three LCS(L)s at those stations. Additionally, on April 11, the IJN sent 30 kamikazes after TF58, operating northeast of Okinawa.

Mitscher received warning of the attack from the boasting of a captured kamikaze pilot. He therefore canceled bombing operations that day, while doubling CAP over the carriers and TF58's picket destroyers. Regardless, a few kamikazes recorded successful hits. The Fletcher-class *Kidd* and *Bullard*, radar pickets, were damaged by one strike, and the battleship *Missouri* had its paint scorched by a direct hit which did little damage. The *Enterprise* suffered flight deck damage, interrupting flight operations for 48 hours, and the *Essex* took minor damage from a near-miss.

*Kikusui* 2 began on April 12, proving wrong Turner's prediction the Japanese had quit the war in the Okinawa sector. Over two days, 185 kamikazes – two-thirds of which the IJN provided – launched attacks. While just half the size of *Kikusui* 1, it was followed up on April 15 and 16 by *Kikusui* 3 with 165 kamikazes. The kamikazes of *Kikusui* 2 were accompanied by 150 fighters and 45 torpedo bombers, whereas *Kikusui* 3 was supplemented by 280 conventional aircraft. Combined, the two later operations equaled *Kikusui* 1, spread over five days.

A new moon and clear weather marked April 12. The Japanese threw everything at the Allied fleet, including Ohka bombs. As in previous *kikusui*, the bulk of the attacks fell on the radar picket stations. The destroyer *Mannert L. Abele* at Picket Station 14 became the first ship hit and the only one sunk by an *Ohka*. The destroyer-minesweeper *Jeffers* at Picket Station 12 was missed by an Ohka before steaming to help rescue *Abele* survivors.

Kamikazes managed almost a clean sweep of the ships at Picket Station 1, heavily damaging the destroyers *Cassin Young* and *Purdy*, sinking LCS(L)-33, and damaging LCS(L)-57. The two remaining LCS(L)s at that station rescued survivors and aided the damaged ships. After repairs, the *Cassin Young* rejoined the war on May 31, but *Purdy*'s repairs were only completed after the war's end.

The destroyer *Stanly*, at Picket Station 2, was hit in the bow by an Ohka that passed through the ship before exploding on the other side. A second Ohka missed, but came close enough to tear off *Stanly*'s ensign. Its damage was patched up at Kerama Retto. An LSM was also damaged by an Ohka at another radar picket station.

Although the kamikazes spent most of their effort on the radar picket stations, some hit the Hagushi beachhead, damaging a cargo ship. Others found the bombardment group, hitting the destroyer *Zellars* and battleship *Tennessee* while having near misses against several other ships in the unit. Other kamikazes attacked Kerama Retto. In all, 16 ships were hit that day. In exchange, Allied fighters and antiaircraft fire downed nearly 300 attacking aircraft during *Kikusui* 2 and 3.

*Kikusui* 3 followed the pattern set by *Kikusui* 2, concentrating on the radar pickets. Eleven ships were hit, with one, the destroyer *Pringle*, sunk while on picket duty. The main attack fell on the second day, when the *Pringle* was sunk. A second destroyer, USS *Laffey*, survived attacks by no fewer than 22 kamikazes. Kerama Retto, Hagushi, and TF58 were also hit, with the *Missouri* and *Intrepid* damaged.

Radar picket losses dropped after *Kikusui* 3, with land-based radar stations on Ie Shima and Hedo Saki starting to operate from April 16. This allowed the

The Essex-class *Bunker Hill* was less fortunate than the *Missouri* on May 11. A kamikaze struck, creating such damage that the Essex-class carrier was still under repair when the war ended. (AC)

number of radar picket stations to be reduced to five, eliminating the most exposed stations to the north of Okinawa.

One more *kikusui* took place in April, *Kikusui* 4, on the 27th and 28th. This was significantly smaller than earlier waves, with only 115 kamikazes, but it succeeded in sinking ammunition ship *Canada Victory* off Hagushi and damaging eight other ships. Most of the latter were destroyers, destroyer conversions, or destroyer escorts at the remaining radar picket stations. However, kamikazes also hit the hospital ship *Solace* and casualty evacuation transport *Pinkney*.

Two further *kikusui* followed in the first two weeks of May, *Kikusui* 5 (May 3–4) and *Kikusui* 6 (May 10–11). *Kikusui* 5 comprised 125 kamikazes, with 75 from the Navy and 50 from the Army, while *Kikusui* 6 had 70 Navy and 80 Army kamikazes. The two waves of kamikazes followed part of the pattern seen in the earlier waves by focusing on ships at the radar picket stations.

Several spectacular battles took place around the picket destroyers and destroyer escorts during these *kikusui*, with waves of kamikazes attacking an individual picket. *Kikusui* 5 was the deadliest since *Kikusui* 3, with three destroyers and three LSMs sunk in this wave. Six more picket ships were damaged during *Kikusui* 6, including the destroyer *Hugh W. Hadley*. Hit by an Ohka, it limped back to the West Coast, but was discarded as a constructive total loss in October 1945.

These *kikusui* also went after the fast carriers in both TF57 and TF58. In TF58, the carriers *Bunker Hill* and *Enterprise* were both damaged by kamikazes, the *Bunker Hill* badly enough that it was still under repair when the war ended. The *Enterprise* only just finished its repairs by August. To the south, covering Sakishimo Gunto, TF57 became the focus of attention. HMS *Formidable* and HMS *Indomitable* were both struck by kamikazes on May 4, while HMS *Victorious* was hit on May 9. In all these cases, the British carriers' armored flight decks prevented serious damage, although the *Formidable* had to withdraw to replenish its air group, which was largely destroyed on deck by a kamikaze strike.

While kamikaze attacks surged during the *kikusui*, kamikazes attacked almost every day between these waves. These individual attacks were often more effective than the mass attacks, since they could come without warning. Ships were damaged and sunk on a daily basis in the waters around Okinawa in April and May.

By mid-May, the kamikaze offensive was faltering. New Allied airfields in Okinawa and Ie Shima permitted long-range USAAF fighters to attack Japanese airfields in Kyushu. It was

The Ohkas made their first hit – and only kill – three weeks after their first use. On April 12, 1945, the Allen B. Sumner-class destroyer *Mannert L. Abele* was hit and sunk by an Ohka while stationed at Radar Picket Station 14 off Okinawa. (USNHHC)

# The Ordeal of USS *Laffey*: Kikusui 3 – April 16, 1945

Radar picket stations were posts of supreme danger during Okinawa. Kamikazes unwilling to push beyond the first ship sighted subjected them to frequent attack. The best example was the ordeal of USS *Laffey* (DD- DD-724). It withstood attacks by 22 aircraft in 80 minutes on the morning of 16 April, 1945.

## Japanese Units:

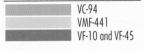

Japanese aircraft
Ki-36 aircraft breaking off attack

## US Units:

VC-94
VMF-441
VF-10 and VF-45

5

2

7

4

8

3

*Laffey*

*LCM(L)-51*

6

## EVENTS

**1.** 0808: *Laffey* detects incoming kamikazes, and requests air cover. Wildcats from *Shamrock Bay* are scrambled. Incoming aircraft become too numerous to count.

**2.** 0828: Ki-36 from Shinbu Unit No. 40 driven off after conducting reconnaissance.

**3.** 0830–0950: *Laffey* comes under kamikaze attack, with 22 aircraft attacking (see inset for sequence of attacks).

**4.** 0846: Four VC-94 Wildcats arrive.

**5.** 0848–0910: VC-94 Wildcats engage and drive off 20 potential kamikazes, shooting down six.

**6.** 0900: Twelve VMF-441 Corsairs arrive.

**7.** 0900–0950: VMF-441 Corsairs engage Japanese aircraft, driving off at least ten more attackers.

**8.** 0910: VC-94 Wildcats breakoff due to low fuel and ammunition.

**9.** 1000: VF-10 F4Us from *Intrepid* and VF-45 Hellcats from *San Jacinto* arrive to take over combat air patrol over *Laffey* and Radar Patrol Station 1. By then, attacks have ceased.

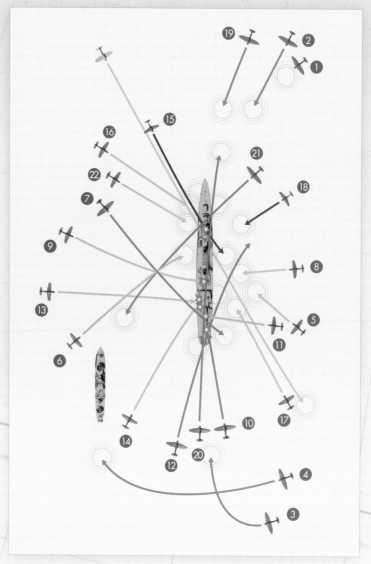

**Inset Key (numbers indicate the order of attacks)**

Corsair
Val
Judy
Oscar

USS *Laffey* after it suffered attacks by 22 Japanese kamikazes. Almost as many kamikazes were prevented from attacking the *Laffey* by fighter cover and antiaircraft fire. The *Laffey* may have absorbed the attention of one-third of the kamikazes dispatched that day. (USNHHC)

Japan used so many aircraft as kamikazes at Okinawa that it was eventually reduced to using primary trainers, such as the Tachikawa Ki-9 biplanes. These proved unexpectedly dangerous because their wood and canvas construction were virtually invisible to radar, including proximity fuze radars. (AC)

not continuous "Big Blue Blanket" coverage, but it significantly reduced Japan's ability to launch kamikaze strikes. The fighter sweeps increased as the need to provide close air support to ground troops on Okinawa diminished. Ground troops were mopping up from mid-May to mid-July, when Okinawa was finally secured. However, all this only marginally reduced *Kikusui* 7, which ran from May 25–28 with 165 kamikazes, managing to sink, cripple, or damage 13 ships.

These attacks came in small groups. Flying low, most managed to avoid radar pickets, and some reached the fire support area. Just after midnight on May 25, two kamikazes struck the old destroyer transport *Barry*, damaging it to the point it was decommissioned and repurposed as a kamikaze decoy. From morning to early afternoon, heavy attacks occurred, sinking *LSM-135* and the high speed transport *Bates*, also damaging three destroyers, two destroyer escorts, two fast destroyer-transports, two mine warfare ships, and an LSC. None of these craft displaced more than 2200 tons, and all were easily replaced.

*Kikusui* 8 ran from May 27–28 and involved 110 kamikazes, split almost evenly between Navy and Army aircraft. It began by attacking the Fifth Fleet and ended targeting the Third Fleet. Halsey

and McCain relieved Spruance and Mitscher on May 27, as the Allies began preparations for the invasion of Japan, Okinawa having been largely secured. Attacking at night and aided by a full moon and 50 percent overcast, *Kikusui* 8 damaged three cargo ships and one transport on May 28. None were seriously damaged however, a pitiful result for the lives expended.

*Kikusui* 9 spanned June 3–7 and comprised only 50 kamikazes. It failed utterly, with CAP or antiaircraft fire shooting down all aircraft involved. In exchange, the *Anthony* was slightly damaged when a Zero it destroyed exploded over the Fletcher-class destroyer, showering it with flaming debris. The *Anthony* was at Picket Station 1, which experienced most of the attacks. A lone non-*kikusui* kamikaze, a D3A, was more successful on June 10 when it struck and sank the destroyer *William D. Porter* at Picket Station 15.

*Kikusui* 10 fared little better. Running between June 21 and 22, it involved 45 kamikazes. One group penetrated Kerama Retto and damaged two seaplane tenders, one seriously. Another group attacked *LSM-59*, towing the decommissioned hulk of the *Barry*, and sank both. With that, Ugaki ended the *kikusui* to hoard Japan's remaining aircraft for use against the Allied invaders when they attacked the Home Islands.

Kamikazes made brief appearances in July and August, when the Third Fleet launched carrier strikes on the Home Islands. Small, occasional raids were also launched against Okinawa during those months, generally by pilots intent on dying for the emperor. The last such attack occurred on August 13, when two kamikazes hit and damaged the attack transport *La Grange* in Buckner Bay.

# Dawn launch

As April 1945 stretched into May, Japan ran short of its usual kamikaze aircraft – the Mitsubishi Zero, Nakajima Hayabusa, Yokosuka Suisei, and Kawasaki Hein – being forced to substitute other aircraft, typically obsolescent light bombers, attack aircraft, and fighters. Eventually, even ancient wood-and-canvas biplane primary trainers were pressed into kamikaze duties.

All were designed prior to World War II, beginning their production in the 1930s. With fixed landing gear slowing them, they were flown by novice pilots, often with less than 100 hours of flight training.

They could not survive long in the combat environment of 1945, but they did not need to. They needed to last only long enough to complete one mission – or by Allied standards, half a mission. They did not need to return. All except the primary trainers could carry a 250kg or 500kg bomb. The primary trainers could carry a 40-gallon drum filled with gasoline or explosives in the second seat. This was enough, it was believed, to sink or at least severely damage an Allied warship or transport.

This plate recreates a scene that would have reoccurred throughout April, May, and June 1945: kamikaze pilots departing on a morning launch from an airfield to strike Allied naval forces around Okinawa. It is a grass field in Kyushu. Its identity is unimportant; the Japanese used grass airstrips throughout southern Kyushu to disperse their aircraft and increase the difficulty of the B-29s attempting to bomb out airfields fielding kamikazes. These fields had primitive fuel and maintenance facilities, but that did not matter as the aircraft only needed enough maintenance to make one flight.

In the air can be seen a pair of Ki-9 primary trainers, each with an explosive-filled fuel drum in the back seat. As slow and vulnerable as they were, they had one advantage over more modern aircraft: they were virtually invisible to radar. They thus had a good chance of slipping in undetected until they came within visual range of Allied ships. Even then, they had an advantage as they were difficult for proximity fuzes to detect. A direct hit was required to knock them down.

Taking off is a Ki-26 fighter carrying a 250kg bomb. Replaced by the Hayabusa in 1940, these aircraft were used as advanced trainers or were seconded to Japanese allies such as Manchukuo or Siam during the Pacific War. Short of other aircraft, they were pressed into service as kamikazes.

Behind it, on the runway awaiting takeoff, is a Ki-36 carrying a 500kg bomb. It was designed as an army cooperation aircraft, providing artillery spotting, reconnaissance, and close air-ground support for the IJA's troops. It proved so vulnerable it was withdrawn from combat in 1942, but now it is being sent on one more mission.

Along the side of the runway, a line of kamikaze pilots can be seen. Awaiting their turn to die for Japan sometime in the near future, they are cheering the pilots departing this day. In a few days, someone else will cheer for them as they depart on their final mission.

## *Downfall*: June 30, 1944–March 1946

Despite defeat at Okinawa, surrender remained unthinkable to the Japanese. But with the Allies firmly lodged on Okinawa, both sides realized the Home Islands were next and planned accordingly.

The Allied plan, *Downfall*, envisioned two operations: *Olympic*, an invasion of the southernmost main island of Kyushu, and *Coronet*, a landing on Honshu near the Japanese capital, Tokyo. *Olympic*, to be executed in November, projected capturing Kyushu's southern half, to permit airfields within range of the Honshu landing beaches. *Coronet* proposed multi-army corps landings on Honshu's east coast north and south of Tokyo. Tokyo's envelopment and capture would follow, with (presumably) surrender once the capital (and possibly emperor) was in Allied hands.

The Japanese defensive plan was labelled *Ketsu* (Decisive). It envisioned repelling a Kyushu invasion, or failing that, making Allied success so costly they would be deterred from further invasions and end the war with a negotiated peace. Japanese planners accurately predicted the main landings were set for Shibushi Bay, the Miyazaki coast, or the Satsuma Peninsula, and planned their defenses accordingly.

Japan intended to blunt these landings with an all-out air assault. The Sixth Air Army, commanded by Lieutenant Genenral Sugawara Michio, and the Fifth Air Fleet under Vice Admiral Ugaki Matome were stationed in Kyushu and could attack immediately. These would be reinforced by the First and Fifth Air Divisions and the Third and Tenth Air Fleets. A joint Army–Navy command was implemented, with inter-service rivalries set aside. The IJN would conduct all long-range and night reconnaissance, with the IJA conducting most short range reconnaissance. All offshore waters off Kyushu to a distance of 600nmi would be covered.

Once the invasion fleet was detected, it would be attacked. To prevent aircraft carriers from supporting the landings, they would be attacked by a picked force of 330 naval aircraft manned by the best pilots still available (surviving veterans of prior combat), reinforced by Army aircraft. These would total 400 to 450 Army aircraft. To further reduce Allied air power, 1,200 airborne troops would be loaded into transport aircraft to attack airfields in Okinawa. The transports would crash-land on the runways, with the debarked troops attacking and disabling the airfields' aircraft and facilities.

Another 250 aircraft were reserved to attack shore bombardment warships, battleships, and heavy cruisers. The remaining Japanese aircraft were to be thrown against troop transports, preferably before they unloaded troops. Round-the-clock attacks were planned, spread over a ten-day period, and all remaining aircraft would be expended.

All these would end up as *tokko* attacks. The airborne troops were to fight to the death. Aircraft making conventional torpedo bombing attacks would finish up by crashing into enemy ships, doubling the damage done. Escorting fighters, once attack aircraft had completed their attacks,

An Ohka captured at Okinawa is displayed. Had Operation *Downfall* occurred, Japan planned to launch them from ground-based cradles at the invasion beaches to counter Allied landings. (USNHHC)

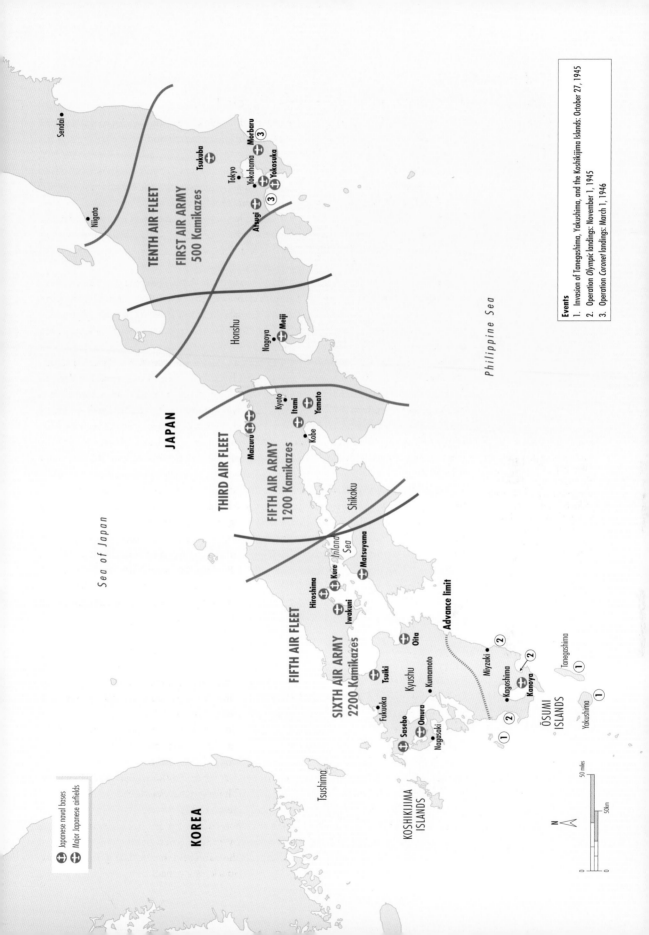

**KOREA**

Tsushima

*Sea of Japan*

**JAPAN**

Niigata •

Sendai •

Honshu

**TENTH AIR FLEET**

**FIRST AIR ARMY**
**500 Kamikazes**

Tsukuba ✈

Morbaru ✈
② Yokahama ✈
Tokyo • ✈ Yokosuka
③ Atsugi ✈

Nagoya • ✈ Meiji

**THIRD AIR FLEET**

Maizuru ✈
Kyoto •
✈ Itami
Kobe • ✈ Yamato

**FIFTH AIR ARMY**
**1200 Kamikazes**

*Inland Sea*
Shikoku

*Philippine Sea*

**FIFTH AIR FLEET**

Hiroshima ✈
Kure ✈
✈ Matsuyama

Iwakuni ✈

**SIXTH AIR ARMY**
**2200 Kamikazes**

✈ Oita

Fukuoka •
Tsuiki ✈
Kyushu
Kumamoto •

Sasebo ✈
Omura ✈
Nagasaki •

Miyzaki •
② Kagoshima •
② Kanoya ✈

**Advance limit**

① ②

① Tanegashima

① Yokushima

**ŌSUMI**
**ISLANDS**

**KOSHIKIJIMA**
**ISLANDS**

Japanese naval bases ✈
Major Japanese airfields ✈

N

0 ____ 50 miles
0 __ 50 km

**Events**

1. Invasion of Tanegashima, Yakushima, and the Koshikijima Islands: October 27, 1945
2. Operation *Olympic* landings: November 1, 1945
3. Operation *Coronet* landings: March 1, 1946

By July 1945, the F8F Bearcat was appearing on US aircraft carriers. More capable than the F6F, it would have made a formidable kamikaze hunter in the invasion of Kyushu had Operation *Olympic* been required. (AC)

were to conclude by diving into a suitable target, namely an aircraft carrier or a transport.

But how many *tokko* would be available? Both the Army and Navy planned to convert every available suitable aircraft into a *tokko*. By the war's end, the air forces had 5,350 conventional combat aircraft available between them. This total included fighters for air defense and long-range reconnaissance aircraft. Another 900 had been converted to kamikaze service, including available Ohkas and Ki-115s, built as suicide aircraft. To this they could add 1,750 advance trainers and 2,700 primary trainers for a total of 10,700 potential kamikazes.

By November, it was believed they might be able to add several hundred more Ohkas and Ki-115s each. However, such a projection was overly optimistic. Japanese aircraft production collapsed in August, and likely would have dropped further in September and October. Even the 10,700 aircraft total was optimistic, as at least 30 percent of combat aircraft were unserviceable, while trainers had to be converted to carry bombs to be effective kamikazes. A more realistic estimate would have been 2,200 aircraft available as kamikazes in Kyushu, with 1,200 reinforcements in Shikoku and western Honshu. Another 900 could potentially have been drawn from northern Honshu and Hokkaido.

To counter "Big Blue Blanket" tactics, the Japanese dispersed kamikaze aircraft throughout Kyushu. Improved airfields were avoided whenever possible. Viewed as targets for Allied airstrikes, the Japanese placed dummy aircraft made of lathe and straw there. Aircraft were instead located in unimproved fields long enough to permit takeoff, but not allow landings. To conceal aircraft, underground hangars were dug.

Some aircraft were based on the shore and concealed in caves, intended to take off from beaches. These included the Ohkas, mounted on launching cradles, eliminating the need for carrier aircraft. They were to wait until the transports were within view and then launch at them.

The scope of the kamikaze effort, even at the numbers planned by Japan, was too small to have any expectation of success. However impressive sending 450 aircraft against the Allied carriers might have sounded, the Allied invasion force would have contained at least 12 US fleet and eight US light carriers, six British fleet and light carriers, and at least 36 escort carriers. These would have carried at least 2,200 fighters of all types, including high-performance Seafires and the new F8F Bearcats. The Allies backed up their fighters with a well-tested integrated air defense system incorporating radar and heavy antiaircraft artillery, along with fighters.

Japanese plans were contingent on saturating the Allied air defenses, which required coordinated launches of multiple aircraft at widely dispersed and primitive airfields using improvised communications. The Allies would have preceded landings with fighter sweeps, beginning before dawn and continuing throughout the day, so individual Japanese aircraft would have been picked off before they could form into mass attacks.

Operation *Olympic* would have most likely ended the kamikaze campaign. Japan's air leaders intended to throw every available aircraft into this struggle. By the time the Allies secured the southern end of Kyushu – they never intended to occupy all of it – there would have been no Japanese aerial forces still in existence. Kamikazes could not have seriously opposed the Honshu landings despite any remaining desire to do so.

# AFTERMATH AND ANALYSIS

The *Downfall* portion of the kamikaze campaign never occurred. It was just as well: it would have been bloody – for both sides. It would have almost certainly failed. Kamikazes would have inflicted ghastly casualties, but Allied planners expected high losses. In anticipation of extremely heavy casualties, the United States stockpiled so many Purple Heart medals (awarded to those injured in combat) that they lasted into the 21st century.

The atomic bombs dropped on Hiroshima and Nagasaki prompted a Japanese surrender. They were little different in outcome to the massive fire raids that had been experienced over the past five months, but the novelty – and horror – of the single weapons permitted the war to end.

Following the fall of the Marianas, Japan's defeat was inevitable. Since then, Japan's war leaders had been ignoring the emperor's desires to end the conflict – even at terms unfavorable to Japan and the emperor – for over a year. They also ignored his reluctance to employ *tokko* tactics, using his admiration of the kamikazes' individual courage as justification for continuing and expanding the campaign. But the emperor seized on Hiroshima and Nagasaki to force his leaders to end the war.

Even then, it was a close-run thing. Junior officers attempted a coup to replace their superiors with those willing to continue the war. They justified their action on the grounds that surrender would disgrace the emperor, that surrender was being forced upon him. Their rebellion was crushed, but just barely.

The surrender led to a wave of suicides by kamikaze leaders. Ugaki flew a kamikaze mission on August 15 after hearing of the impending surrender, arguing he could do this because he had not yet received formal orders to surrender. Others followed suit, either flying to oblivion or committing suicide as atonement.

Ōnishi Takijirō committed *seppuku*, a ritualistic suicide in which he disemboweled himself with his sword, the following day. He did so to atone for starting the kamikaze campaign. He felt it was his only adequate apology to the 4,000-odd kamikazes sent to their deaths on his initiative, and to their families thus deprived of a son, husband,

A kamikaze, in this case an Achi D3A dive bomber, is caught and shot down by a Navy fighter before it can reach its target. Ill-trained Japanese kamikaze pilots proved easy kills. In this case, the interceptor is an F4F Wildcat providing cover for an escort carrier task group. (AC)

A kamikaze is hit and set ablaze by US Navy antiaircraft fire before it can reach USS *Hornet* on March 18, 1945. Allied antiaircraft capability was one of three major factors leading to the downfall of Japan's attempt to use kamikazes to stop the Allied advance. (AC)

father, brother, or cousin. He refused a second who traditionally ends the suffering of the *seppuku* practitioner after the fatal wound is inflicted. He took 15 painful hours to die.

It was, perhaps, fitting. Ōnishi's assessment was correct: the kamikazes' sacrifices had been in vain. By any objective measure, the kamikaze campaign was an utter failure. It did not prevent the Allied occupation of Japan, and would not have deterred an Allied invasion of the Home Islands. It hardly slowed the final Allied advances, as logistics rather than the kamikazes dictated their pace.

In Ōnishi's defense, he was a reluctant adopter of kamikaze. He implemented it only after it was thrust on him by a deceased predecessor and due to the urgings of subordinates, whose number included pilots intended to conduct *tokko* missions.

At first, kamikaze seemed to offered real promise. The initial wave of suicide attackers reaped a high return on investment. Well over one-third of these attacks yielded damage to Allied ships, with ten percent of ships hit sinking. This was a real threat to the Allies. Total damage inflicted was limited because these attacks were a pilot program, a feasibility study, which led to the program's expansion.

Success was largely a product of surprise. Throughout November 1944, the US Navy began experimenting with countermeasures. By December 1, the Navy's fleets had in place a set of integrated defenses against kamikazes. These included modified CAP procedures, picket warships, increasing fighters carried aboard fleet carriers, and accelerating introduction of the proximity-fuzed antiaircraft shells.

Results appeared immediately: by the end of the Allies' Philippine campaigns in January 1945, damage effectiveness dropped dramatically. Taken as a whole, only 27 percent of all kamikazes expended in the Philippines managed to land a damaging blow, with an overall sinking effectiveness of 2.9 percent. This dropped even more conspicuously during the struggle for Okinawa, where only 15 percent of kamikazes damaged enemy warships and less than ten percent of these attacks resulted in an actual sinking.

In a very real sense, the Allies won the kamikaze campaign by the end of January, despite the larger amount of casualties they incurred after that. Although the Allies did not yet realize they had won, Japan did. By the time they withdrew aircraft from the Philippines, the Japanese knew kamikazes could not stop the Allies.

During the campaign, approximately 350 vessels were hit by kamikazes. Of these, around 47 were sunk and 300 damaged. Of the ships sunk, three were escort carriers and six were large cargo ships (Liberty or Victory ships). The rest were minor vessels: 13 destroyers, 18 amphibious warfare ships (landing ships or craft and destroyer transport conversions), two patrol torpedo boats, one subchaser, and four miscellaneous auxiliary warships (mine warfare or tugs). All were strategically unimportant vessels, even the escort carriers. All could be easily replaced.

Of the ships damaged, only that done to aircraft carriers had the potential to derail the Allied offensive. They were particularly vulnerable to kamikazes, as the wooden flight decks of the US carriers were easily penetrated by kamikazes and all carriers operated aircraft loaded with aviation fuel and explosives. Thirty-one different aircraft carriers were damaged on 39 separate occasions: 14 fleet carriers (including two Royal Navy ships), three light carriers, and 14 escort carriers.

Several, including the *Bunker Hill*, *Enterprise*, *Franklin*, and *Saratoga*, were damaged badly enough to require long stays in repair yards. USS *Franklin* earned the dubious distinction of being the most heavily damaged fleet carrier of the war, superb damage control allowing it to survive damage significantly more severe than that which sank the *Lexington*, *Yorktown*, or *Hornet* in 1942. It would not complete repairs until 1946.

At no point were enough fast carriers damaged to threaten or even restrict Fast Carrier Task Force operations. Furthermore, the armored flight decks of the British carriers meant damage to them was minor. Similarly, by 1945 so many escort carriers had been built that the only result of kamikaze damage to escort carriers was to reduce the pool of surplus carriers.

Kamikazes hit 11 different battleships and 12 different cruisers over the course of the kamikaze campaign. None of the battleships were seriously damaged. In several cases, damage consisted only of burned paint. Similarly, with the exception of the ancient *Australia* (hit on four separate occasions by kamikazes), no cruiser suffered damage sufficient to end its naval career. Most were in action at the war's end.

Forty-five large cargo ships or troop transports were damaged over the course of the campaign. Damage ranged from very light (in one case a cargo boom destroyed by a kamikaze) to a ship being reduced to a constructive total loss. Sometimes, even badly damaged ships remained useful. A ship immobilized by engine damage could be used as a floating warehouse in places like Kerama Retto which lacked other storage. Since over 3,500 of these types of cargo vessels were constructed during World War II, even if all transports hit by kamikazes had sunk, it would have had little effect.

The bulk of the kamikazes' wrath fell on minor vessels. Almost half of the ships damaged were destroyers, destroyer escorts, or different auxiliary warships converted from destroyers. Another 30 were amphibious warfare ships. Most, including the destroyer conversions, were serving on picket stations when they were damaged.

A second major reason for the defeat of the kamikazes was Allied radar and radio communications. They contributed to an integrated air defense system which permitted early detection of incoming threats and allowed timely interception of "bandits." (AC)

Allied damage control was a third factor leading to the kamikazes' downfall. Allied firefighting capabilities dampened the greatest threat a kamikaze strike posed, while damage control crews could quickly and effectively repair even severe damage, like this hole in an escort carrier's flight deck. (AC)

This was achieved at a cost of approximately 2,600 aircraft expended as kamikazes and at least as many lost supporting such missions. The more important loss was that of the 4,000 airmen killed as kamikazes. They were exactly the young men Japan most needed to rebuild after the war's end: patriotic, courageous, and willing to do anything for Japan.

Perhaps the most disturbing aspect of the kamikaze campaign once Japan's high command committed to *tokko* was the ad hoc nature of Japanese planning. Japan fought the kamikaze campaign on interior lines and short supply lines, historically a route to victory. Interior lines allow the attacker to concentrate their attack at the enemy's weakest point, while an enemy, with converging columns and lengthening supply lines, has difficulty moving reinforcements to the point of the attack.

There was no coordinated attempt to use these advantages. The Imperial Japanese Army and Navy failed to cooperate with each other, initially seeing it more as an inter-service competition than a campaign to defeat an enemy. Demonstrating the willingness of pilots of their own service to make the supreme sacrifice for their emperor and nation seemed more important than getting the greatest possible return on that sacrifice.

Neither the Imperial General Headquarters nor the individual commanders of the Army and Navy put much thought into using kamikazes. There was no study of how to use them most effectively. Worse still, tactical studies were limited to maximizing the chance of a hit rather than maximizing the damage done. The mission was seemingly accomplished by the pilot's sacrifice.

Most ships sank due to loss of watertight integrity, but little thought was given to tactics that would increase the opportunity to cause such damage. Yet even aircraft armed with heavy bombloads, including heavy twin-engine bombers carrying 1,600kg (3,600lb) of explosives, carried contact fuzes, ensuring most of the damage would occur above the waterline and on the superstructure.

## Surviving aircraft and ships

For obvious reasons, no Japanese aircraft used as kamikazes survived. Even examples of the types of aircraft employed in kamikaze duty are scarce because relatively few Japanese military aircraft survived World War II. Most consist of bits of different aircraft pieced together to form one complete aircraft.

Of the most commonly used kamikaze aircraft, the A6M Zero, some 30 still exist. There are also a few replicas. Of the other aircraft often used as kamikazes, two D4Ys, three D3As, one P1Y, two Ki-27s, five Ki-43s, and one Ki-84 survive. Most are not flyable, and some are not on display. Most are in museums in Japan and the United States. No Ki-27s are known to exist; nor do aircraft modified to kamikaze duty, such as the twin-engine K-48s and Ki-67s.

Eighteen examples of the Yokosuka MXY-7 Ohka still exist, of the 850-plus built. This is unsurprising considering the fascination these aircraft held for the Allies. Japan's former enemies hold 16 of these: one in India, four in the UK, and 11 in the United States. All are currently on display in museums in their respective countries. The other two survivors are in Japanese museums. All are on static display, with none maintained in flying condition.

Only two of the never-used Nakajima Ki-115 suicide aircraft survive of the 105 completed before Japan's surrender brought an end to production. One is in the United States, on display at the Pima Air and Space Museum, along with an Ohka. A second became a gate guardian at Yokota Air Base. In 1952, the USAF returned it to the Japanese government. It is now reportedly on display in a Japanese museum.

There are many more surviving examples of the types of Allied aircraft that fought the kamikazes, including some that are flyable. This is largely because the Allies won, and the late-war variants of the participating aircraft were far more likely to survive during postwar years.

Thirty-one Wildcats still exist, most of them the various FM types built by General Motors and flown off escort carriers during 1944 and 1945. The majority are in the United States, including 15 airworthy examples. There are also 31 surviving F6F Hellcats, with one in Britain and the rest in the United States. Sixteen are airworthy and 14 under restoration. Some 60 F4Us survive, 45 of them in the United States, including 26 that are airworthy. This total includes several postwar aircraft which could not have participated in the kamikaze campaign, but which are representative of those that did. Six Seafires survive, including two flyable examples in the UK and two on static display at UK museums.

For those interested in seeing the most different types of aircraft that participated – Japanese and Allied – the best choice seems to be the Pima Air and Space Museum in Tucson, Arizona.

Several victims of kamikazes remain, including the *Missouri*, preserved at Pearl Harbor, and the Fletcher-class destroyers *Cassin Young* and *Kidd*. The *Cassin Young* is now part of Boston National Historical Park, in Massachusetts, and the *Kidd* is in Baton Rouge, Louisiana. All three ships are open to visitors.

One of two surviving examples of the Ki-115 suicide plane is on display at the Pima Air and Space Museum in Tucson, Arizona. Note the bolt-on landing gear which was to be jettisoned after takeoff. (Courtesy of Pima Air and Space Museum)

# FURTHER READING

As with most of these books, assembling the information to write it was like solving a jigsaw puzzle. No one source had everything, and often I pulled only a few bits of critical information from the several hundred sources I used. Additionally, many of the popular histories of the kamikaze campaign focus on the tactical aspects – the pilots and aircraft. This is understandable, as they offer a compelling story, while the strategic aspects are often confusing. Of the recent popular histories, one I would recommend is *Rain of Steel* by Stephen L. Moore (Naval Institute Press, Annapolis MD, 2020). Its main focus is the Okinawa phase.

For the Allied side, my primary sources came from service histories: Morison's three volumes covering the end of the Pacific War, Roskill's third volume in his Royal Navy History, and Craven and Cate's fifth volume in their Army Air Force series. For the Japanese side, I drew on MacArthur's report on the Pacific War, using a volume relating the war from the Japanese side, and several US Strategic Bombing Survey reports, especially their volume *Japanese Air Power*.

The bibliography below represents a list of the most significant sources. Asterisked sources are available online.

Craven, Wesley Frank & Cate, James Lea (editors), *The Army Air Forces in World War II, Volume Five: The Pacific: Matterhorn to Nagasaki, June 1944 to August 1945*, Office of Air Force History, Washington, DC (1983).*

Hobbs, David (editor), "The British Pacific Fleet in 1945" in *The Commonwealth Navies: 100 Years of Cooperation, 2009 King-Hall Naval History Conference Proceedings*, Sea Power Centre – Australia, Canberra, Australia (2012).*

MacArthur, Douglas & Willoughby, Charles Andrew, *Japanese Operations in the Southwest Pacific Area. Volume II. Part II*, US Government Printing Office, Washington, DC (1966).*

Morison, Samuel Eliot, *History of United States Naval Operations in World War II, Volume XII: Leyte: June 1944 – January 1945*, Little, Brown, Boston, Mass (1958).

Morison, Samuel Eliot, *History of United States Naval Operations in World War II, Volume XIII: The Liberation of the Philippines: Luzon, Mindanao, the Visayas: 1944–1945*, Little, Brown, Boston, Mass (1959).

Morison, Samuel Eliot, *History of United States Naval Operations in World War II, Volume XIV: Victory in the Pacific: 1945*, Little, Brown, Boston, Mass (1960).

Roskill, S. W., *History of the Second World War, War at Sea, 1939–45: The Offensive v. 3*, Her Majesty's Stationary Office, London (1960–62).

United States Fleet, Headquarters of the Commander in Chief, *Anti-Suicide Action Summary August 1945*, Navy Department, Washington, DC (1945).

United States Fleet, Headquarters of the Commander in Chief, *Battle Experience: Radar Pickets and Methods of Combating Suicide Attacks off Okinawa March–May 1945*, Navy Department, Washington, DC (1945).

United States Strategic Bombing Survey, *Air Campaigns of the Pacific War*, Military Analysis Division, Washington, DC (1947).*

United States Strategic Bombing Survey, *Japanese Air Power*, Naval Analysis Division, Washington, DC (1946).*

United States Strategic Bombing Survey, *The Campaigns of the Pacific War*, Naval Analysis Division, Washington, DC (1946).*

Wallace, Robert, *From Dam Neck to Okinawa: A Memoir of Antiaircraft Training in World War II*, Naval Historical Center, Department of the Navy, Washington, DC (2001).

# INDEX

References to images are in **bold**.